THE ANALYST'S REVERIES

While the use of the analyst's own reveries in work with patients has increased in recent times, there has been little critical inquiry into its value, and the problems it may lead to. *The Analyst's Reveries* finds increasing veneration for the analyst's use of their reveries, while revealing important differences amongst post-Bionians in how reverie is defined and used clinically. Fred Busch ponders if it has been fully recognized that some post-Bionians suggest a new, radical paradigm for what is curative in psychoanalysis.

After searching for the roots of the analyst's use of reverie in Bion's work and questioning whether in this regard Bion was a Bionian, Busch carefully examines the work of some post-Bionians and finds both convincing ways to think about the usefulness and limitations of the analyst's use of reverie. He explores questions including:

- From what part of the mind does a reverie emerge?
- How does its provenance inform its transformative possibilities?
- Do we over-generalize in conceptualizing what is unrepresented, with the corresponding problem of false positives?
- Do dreams equal understanding and what about the generalizability of the co-created reverie?

Busch concludes that it is primarily through the analyst's own associations that the reverie's potential is revealed, which further helps the analyst distinguish it from many other possibilities, including the analyst's countertransference. He believes in the importance of converting reveries into verbal interpretations, a controversial point amongst post-Bionians. Busch ends with the difficult task of classifying the analyst's reveries based on their degree of representation.

The Analyst's Reveries will be of great interest to psychoanalysts and psychoanalytic psychotherapists.

Fred Busch is a Training and Supervising Analyst at the Boston Psychoanalytic Society and Institute, USA. He is the author of *Creating a Psychoanalytic Mind* (Routledge, 2013).

THE ANALYST'S REVERIES

Explorations in Bion's Enigmatic Concept

Fred Busch

30, 32, 34, 66, 75, 76, 80, 81, 82
83, 86, 89, 90, 91

Routledge
Taylor & Francis Group

LONDON AND NEW YORK

First published 2019
by Routledge
2 Park Square, Milton Park, Abingdon, Oxon OX14 4RN

and by Routledge
52 Vanderbilt Avenue, New York, NY 10017

Routledge is an imprint of the Taylor & Francis Group, an informa business

British Library Cataloguing in Publication Data
A catalogue record for this book is available from the British Library

Library of Congress Cataloging-in-Publication Data
A catalog record for this book has been requested

ISBN: 978-0-367-13416-7 (hbk)
ISBN: 978-0-367-13417-4 (pbk)
ISBN: 978-0-429-02635-5 (ebk)

Typeset in Bembo
by Taylor & Francis Books

Printed and bound in Great Britain by
TJ International Ltd, Padstow, Cornwall

For my first reader and editor, always—CSH

CONTENTS

1

THE BEGINNING

In everything I've written to this point, I was pursuing an idea. This book is the result of an *idea pursuing* me. Let me explain.

It all began with a clinical puzzle, leading to a three-year immersion in the work of Bion and the post-Bionions[1] on the analyst's reveries, while also examining my analytic practice to see how and if reveries emerged. The serendipitous event that started this journey occurred in the form of a discussion by Cláudio Eizirik of my keynote paper (Busch, 2015) at the meetings of the International Psychoanalytic Association. His discussion, which centered on a reverie he shared with his patient, at first baffled and then intrigued me. My first inclination was to dismiss its importance, but I found myself coming back to it again and again, leading me to re-think my initial reaction.[2] However, my fascination with how an analyst uses his reveries continued long after the meetings, and this book is the result.

Here is Eizirik's example of how he used an unbidden reverie, the patient's response to it, followed by the train of thoughts I had about it *at the time*.

It was a Monday session. The patient begins to tell me the weekend events, in which he had a quarrel with his parents, and felt distant from his wife and children. He proceeds to a detailed description of each event, and while I listened, in fact nothing came to my mind but boredom, and the feeling that once again the week was beginning with the monotony and the obsessive defenses that are one of his usual retreats. I have nothing to say, nothing to ask, nothing.

Then an image comes to my mind, and I am looking at it, and finding it amusing, apparently forgetting the patient who goes on in his discourse. I imagine two kids in a bathtub, both of them full of soap, in such a way that it is impossible for each of them to grab the other, or hold an arm or the head of the other, in short, there is an absolute impossibility of getting in touch. It seems to me that this describes what is going on in the session. And so, I ask the patient what he would think of a scene that had just occurred to me, and I describe it to him, and ask him whether this could also describe what was going on between the two of us.

After a silence, during which I was afraid I had just said some nonsense, the patient begins to laugh and tells me that this was a common game among he and his brothers in their childhood, nicknamed 'you cannot catch me'. And this opened the way to talk about his defensive maneuvers against a more fluid communication, and to understand that change is never easy, and that we tend to cling to what's familiar to us, what we know about ourselves and our world.

My immediate reaction to hearing Cláudio's reverie was *YIKES! This is way out of the patient's neighborhood,* [3] *and I hope he doesn't share it with the patient.* But he does, and the whole atmosphere in the session changed. How to understand this? Before attempting an answer, let me back up a bit.

If I were capable of creating such an empathic image would I have said it? My first response was *probably not!* Why? As with Cláudio I see the boredom he felt in the session as a result of the patient's defensive enactment in language action[4] to dampen down any excitement in the room. Thus, if I could have the same image as Cláudio, I would try to contain it, and associate to how this image fits with my feelings of boredom in the session. It would not be a big jump to see how boredom could come up as a defense against this image, which could be considered a compromise formation…i.e., nobody is grabbing anything in this exciting bathtub we are in together. We can then see the *detailed, monotonous description of familiar weekend quarrels and distance as a defense* against the wish to grab or be grabbed in the analytic bathtub. So, my first thought was that I would deal with the defense.

That was where my thoughts stopped after my initial reading of Cláudio's example. In fact, though, the more I thought about it, *what upon first impression seemed like two different ways of working, struck me as having several similarities.* That is each of us, in our own way, was trying to bring derivatives of the unconscious into the preconscious. My method was based upon my inclination to analyze the defenses against awareness so that the patient would feel safer to allow in the unconscious derivatives. Cláudio's method is a variant of what some have called, "tickling" the unconscious derivative in the preconscious, thus not diving past what the patient is capable of understanding. In short, we are both concerned with bringing unconscious derivatives to the preconscious. It is my impression Eizerik understood something at the preconscious/unconscious border that led to his *reverie*, without his (Eizirik) awareness of the source. We can see in the patient's animated response, and further associations, that Eizerik's comment touched on something that was on the border of the patient's preconscious/unconscious. If it was deeper in the unconscious we assume it would be unavailable to the patient for an affective change (i.e., too threatening) or further associations.

Bucci's (2001) concept of subsymbolic[5] thinking helps us understand how Eizirik came to his understanding.

The analyst who responds based on his subsymbolic computation, without as yet formulating this in symbolic terms, is nevertheless working with systematic knowledge—subsymbolic "knowing"—not in some magical or primitive mode. There are bases for his inferences that may eventually be identified, although he may not do this in the immediacy of the interaction.

(p. 66)

Inspired and intrigued by Eizirik's example, I began to read further into what to that point had been a vague concept in my mind (i.e., the analyst's reveries). In my early reading of the Bionian literature I began to feel like a Monsieur Jourdain from an adaptation of Molière's *The Bourgeois Gentleman* by Timothy Mooney, who discovered that he has "been speaking prose all my life, and didn't even know it!" That is, I realized I'd been having what some would consider reveries for many years, but classified them under the broader definition of associations or countertransference musings. As I delved further into the topic, the importance of distinguishing between these different forms of the analyst's *knowing* became clearer to me.

Problems in re-thinking a concept

It isn't easy to examine a psychoanalytic concept like the analyst's reveries that has, for many, become an essential component in understanding all our patients, but especially those with early experiences that seem to have been only weakly represented. Like many developments in psychoanalysis, once a concept has shown to be of clinical value, the emphasis becomes one of discovering its utility, and critical inquiry seems to stop. As this happens what gets set aside are significant differences in what the concept means, and how it might best be used clinically. Further, the recent history of psychoanalysis is characterized by a valuable clinical idea soon becoming a separate school, followed by the dismissal of previous ideas of what psychoanalysis is. In my own psychoanalytic lifetime I have seen this with the Kohutians; Relationalists, Interpersonalists; and more recently some of the post-Bionians. As Ferro (Ferro and Nicoli, 2017), referring to Freud's work, recently said: "As far as its clinical use today is concerned it is useless: reading something from Freud is never going to be helpful in the clinical situation" (p. 47).

As I turned my attention to the literature on the analyst's reveries I realized, as Grotstein (Grotstein, 2009) noted, "Of all Bion's new ideas, that of 'reverie' seems to be acquiring the most cachet as an instrument of technique" (p. 69). Even as this was happening, I realized that, as far as I could tell, there hadn't been *an extended inquiry into the concept.* This seemed long overdue, and essential, as the use of reverie is presented by some of the leading post-Bionian thinkers as nothing less than an *entirely new basis for thinking about the methods and goals of treatment.* As recently stated by Ferro (Ferro and Nicoli, 2017) we "have to defend ourselves from what we already know: all that is known should not interest us anymore" (p. 2).

In fact, given what seems like an explosion of interest in reverie over the last decade, I think Grotstein was modest in his claim. While for many years I only cautiously accepted reverie's usefulness, I have come to believe that it has the *potential* to be an important tool available to psychoanalysts in understanding what, to a certain point in treatment, has been *ineffable*. Yet, in using any tool there must be guidelines for the best results. Trying to use an axe to open a jar may accomplish its goal, but it can also lead to unforeseen consequences. In my travels through reverie I found *many inconsistencies in how reveries were defined, and how the term is used in the clinical setting*. Ferro (Ferro and Nicoli, 2017) captured this same phenomenon when he pointed out how reverie has

> spread like wildfire across all conceptualizations of psychoanalysis, so it is one of those umbrella concepts that after a while could mean everything and its opposite, sort of like the term "projective identification", so we can't understand each other.
>
> *(p. 73)*

The answer to basic questions like what a reverie consists of, in what part of the analyst's mind does a reverie form, is it necessary to translate reveries into words, remain elusive. I have attempted to point out the various answers to these questions by post-Bionian analysts, while also formulating some way of how to think about these questions.

The analyst's reveries, as a concept, is not alone in its multiple meanings. Since the very beginning of my clinical inquiries into psychoanalytic concepts (Busch, 1968) what seemed like a well-defined concept was often rife with inconsistencies and multiple ways of understanding (e.g., resistances, working through, countertransference, etc.). While others may despair over such a finding, for someone who likes mysteries, it has most often proven the beginning of an intriguing journey. I think everything I've ever written has something of this quality. In an interview the actor Daniel Day-Lewis, known for his absorption in the roles he plays (e.g., in preparation for playing an enigmatic dress designer in the movie *The Perfect Thread*, he apprenticed under the costume designer for New York City Ballet), described the allure as "discovering something that seems beyond reach, sometimes impossibly beyond reach, that pulls you forward into its orbit somehow."[6] Learning and thinking about the analyst's reveries had something of this quality.

Like any journey into a mystery, though, it is also filled with frustration, especially when the writings of those who subscribe to the importance of a concept sometimes obscure differences to show they are on the same team. It was interesting, then, while writing this essay I came across a comment by the late Oliver Sachs, who said, "Writing is a bulwark against chaos. I have to write to come to terms with experience".[7] While I would probably use the word "confusion" rather than chaos, I think Sachs captured something primal in the experience of honestly immersing oneself in a psychoanalytic concept. This is how I felt in trying to understand the Bionian concept of *reverie*. I read about it, heard people talk about it in discussions and presentations of clinical material, and even thought I used it in my own work. *Yet what it meant remained elusive.* Some might say it is the nature of the term that leads it to remain elusive, however I believe that for us to evaluate the worth of a concept, let alone talk and argue with each other about it, we need to have a certain reliability[8] in how we define a concept. Psychoanalysis has been especially adept at avoiding this principle leading us, at times, to have discussions that come close to a virtual Tower of Babel.

An interesting question was posed by some when reading an early summary of this book...i.e., what happens when a psychoanalyst from one theoretical perspective is trying to immerse himself and discuss a concept from another tradition? Does this work? Can it be constructive?[9] Ferro's (2015) criticism of attempts to understand his work from a Freudian perspective, believing the models were not comparable, is a typical reaction. Ogden (2011) offers a different perspective in his discussion of a paper by Susan Isaacs.

> The important thing is what one is able to do with the ideas Isaacs makes explicit in combination with the ideas that her language suggests...In addition, and probably more important, I have a mind of my own, and that allows me to see in her work a good deal that she did not see. The same is true for you the reader, in reading Isaacs and in reading what I write.
>
> *(p. 4)*

Ogden's need to defend his understanding of Isaacs speaks to a larger issue in psychoanalysis of our tendency to dismiss critics from outside our circle, and thus lose whatever contribution they might make to our understanding.

A further problem in discussing a concept like reverie is that, over time, certain terms become reified. In countering such a view, I believe O'Shaughnessy (2005) said it best when writing about Bion: "Bion's writings are not sacred texts. They are open to criticism and his psychoanalytic writings belong *not to any one of us*, but to the 'systematic ensemble' that is called psychoanalysis" (p. 1527).

Further, it seems to me that all psychoanalysts are attempting to explain the same mind. We use certain methods to listen and understand our patients, and have particular ways of interpreting or not. We have explanatory concepts for our ways of working, and I believe they can, and maybe need to be, compared with other analytic theories on the same issues. Also, I believe there is more common ground along certain lines than Ferro believes (Busch, 2014).

An outline of the book

This book is an attempt to give an informative, but not exhaustive review of Bionian and the post-Bionian views of the analyst's use of reveries. As there are so many definitions of reverie out there, to simplify matters while demonstrating their complexity, I have chosen to focus first on Bion's views, and then mainly three post-Bionions well known for their work: Thomas Ogden; Antonio Ferro; and Elias and Elizabeth da Rocha Barros.[10]

Chapter 2 is a summary of some key definitions to help those not so familiar with Bion's work. Chapters 3 and 4 describe Bion's surprisingly few statements about the analyst's reveries, and what we can tell about his use of the concept. While Bion wrote little about his actual work with patients, he conducted many seminars throughout the world, and there is a report of an analysis with Bion, and from this one can glean his general approach to clinical material. Regarding the analyst's reveries, from the assembled descriptions of Bion's work I ask the question, *was Bion a Bionian?*

Chapter 5 is in some ways the heart of the book. It looks, in detail, at the clinical views of Ogden, Ferro and the da Rocha Barros…their similarities and differences. There are many surprises here. Chapter 6 takes the findings from the previous Chapter and highlights the conceptual problems in how reverie has been used.

At the heart of some post-Bionians' view of reverie is the belief that they are entirely co-constructed. Chapter 7 looks at some of the ethical problems in such a position, and looks at how we can potentially sort out what is our own idiosyncratic reaction to a patient from an empathic co-construction. Chapter 8 attempts to build some conceptual clarity to the thinking about the analyst's reveries by looking at their level of psychic representation, and thus their transformative potential. Whatever way one wants to describe it, the heart of Bion's concept of reverie is that it has the possibility to transform more primitive mental states into potentially representable thoughts.

Notes

1 I am using this term to refer to those Bionian leaning authors who have attempted to define the analyst's use of his reveries in the immediacy of the clinical situation in the last thirty years.

2 This is not the first time Eizirik is cited for a reverie that had an important impact. The Botellas (2013) mention how an acoustic reverie brought up by Eizirik at the Brazilian Congress of Rio de Janeiro in 2006 helped the analyst understand an impasse in treatment.

3 Freud (1910) introduced this metaphor, and I've used it to describe the importance of interpreting to what is close to preconsciously available (Busch, 1993, 2014).

4 A term I've used to describe when words are more like actions, and unconsciously meant to do something.

5 (While) subsymbolic processing is understood scientifically through complex mathematical models (Smolensky, 1988; Rumelhart, 1989) (it) is experientially immediate and familiar to us in the actions and decisions of everyday life—from aiming a piece of paper at a wastebasket or entering a line of moving traffic to feeling that rain is coming, knowing when the pasta is *almost* done and must be drained to be "al dente," and responding to facial expressions or gestures (Bucci, 2001, p.48, italics added)

6 R. Ugwu, *New York Times*, December 2017.

7 As reported by Erica Goode, *New York Times*, September 1, 2015.

8 I am using it here in the scientific sense of replicable.

9 In an article reviewing the concept of countertransference Jacobs (1999) wrote, "I will do so from my own perspective; that is, from the viewpoint of one American analyst, trained in a classical institute… (p.575). My training was like that described by Jacobs, and I have spent the last twenty years immersing myself in the literature not explored in my training, which has led to my view that within certain areas there is a common ground amongst seemingly diverse theoretical perspectives (Busch, 2014, 2015),

10 While this looks suspiciously like there are four authors, not three, I am including the Barros as one, in that they have written together, and have similar ideas about the analyst's use of reverie. Of course, they have written separately about many other topics.

2

THREE DEFINITIONS

For those who have had only a passing interest in the work of Bion and the post-Bionians, here are three definitions of terms that might be unfamiliar. Bion's original definitions are most often elliptical, leading one to get a *sense of something* rather than a more specific characterization.

Beta elements—Bion described beta-elements as *sense-impressions* related to emotional experience. Most analysts would include beta elements amongst more primitive states. "Clinically the bizarre object which is suffused with superego characteristics comes nearest to provide a realization to correspond with the concept of beta elements" (Bion, 1962, p. 26). Ogden (2003) elaborated that

> Beta-elements cannot be linked with one another in the creation of meaning. They might very roughly be compared with 'snow' on a malfunctioning television screen in which no single visual scintillation or group of scintillations can be linked with other scintillations to form an image or even a meaningful pattern. Beta-elements are fit only for evacuation or for storage—not as memory but as psychic noise.
>
> *(p. 17)*

Alpha elements—Elias da Rocha Barros (2000) explained how

> Bion hypothesized a function that he called the *alpha function*, aimed at transforming the beta elements into alpha elements, these latter constituting *the first form of representation* of emotional experience. Emotions thus take on the quality of being thinkable, but they do not yet consist of thoughts. We could characterize such emotions as proto-ideas. If these beta elements fail to be transformed and acquire a thinkable form, according to Bion (1963), they are either expelled from the system by a projective process of an evacuative nature, or they become somatic symptoms.
>
> *(da Rocha Barros, 2000, p. 1008)*

Alpha function—The elliptical nature of Bion's definitions is nowhere more obvious that in his definition of alpha function.

> Alpha-function is the name given to an abstraction used by the analyst to describe a function, of which he does not know the nature, until such time he feels in position to replace it by factors for which he feels he has obtained evidence in the course of the investigation in which he is employing alpha function.
>
> *(Bion, 1962, pgs. 25–26)*

Ogden (2003) went on to describe it as an

> as yet unknown set of mental operations that, together, transform raw sense impressions ('beta-elements') into elements of experience (termed 'alpha-elements') which can be stored as unconscious memory in a form that makes them accessible for creating linkages necessary for unconscious as well as preconscious and conscious psychological work, such as dreaming, thinking, repressing, remembering, forgetting, mourning, reverie and learning from experience.
>
> *(pgs. 17–18)*

I will not comment on these definitions, at this time, as I prefer to discuss them in the larger context of the analyst's reveries.

3

BION'S DEFINITION OF REVERIE

A brief review

While Bion (1962) is referenced by Bionians as the psychoanalytic source of the term reverie and its meaning, the terms *reverie and* (what is often equated with reverie) *waking dreams, were actually first used by* Breuer (1893) in describing his work with Anna O. "She fell into a *waking dream* and saw a black snake coming towards the sick man from the wall to bite him" (p. 38). This was called a "hypnoid state", and described by Breuer as a type of autohypnosis, occurring spontaneously, alternating with more usual waking states. He went on to describe how *reveries* were related to the hypnoid state when he stated, "It seems certain that with her the auto-hypnosis had the way paved for it by habitual *reveries*…" (pgs. 217–218, italics added). Breuer and Freud (1893) equated *daydreams* with *reveries* and linked them to hypnoid states, which "often, it would seem, grow out of the day-dreams which are so common even in healthy people" (p. 13). So some time before Bion's introduction of the term reverie, there is a long psychoanalytic history associated with it. Further, the state of mind described as reveries by Freud and Breuer, were very much like those labeled as reveries by Bionians. Pre-Bion much of the literature on reverie revolved around other functions it may serve (e.g., defensive), and its similarities and differences to other psychic mechanisms (e.g., dissociation). While some recognized that reveries could also occur in the analyst, it was most often labeled as a countertransference problem (Dickes, 1965).

However, what Bion introduced was to *link reverie with the analyst's mind*, and in this way opened a new direction for how an analyst might better understand his patients. Yet, Bion's main contribution to defining reverie is a relatively small contribution of a few paragraphs in his 1962 book, *Learning from Experience*. Ogden (2003) wondered if "'defined' can ever be used with regard to Bion's elusive, evocative, constantly evolving thinking and writing" (p. 17). This quality of Bion's writing has led, on one side, to creative interpretations of what he was trying to elucidate, but on the other side, to multiple definitions, and the underlying psychic states they represent. As we shall see it has resulted in leading post-Bionians defining reverie differently, while overlooking these variances.

With all that has been written about reverie, I think it is worthwhile remembering what Bion said about it, and thus I will quote and reflect on two long quotes that define his views and those that followed. These quotes are the soil upon which later views of reverie were built.

Learning from experience

> Though the difficulties of penetrating the adult mind in analysis are great they are less so than attempting to penetrate the infant's by speculative hypothesis; investigation of reverie in the adult may afford us an entry into this problem. We may deduce from reverie, as the psychological source of supply of the infant's needs for love and understanding, what kind of psychological receptor organ is required if the infant is to be able to profit from reverie as it is able, thanks to the digestive capacities of the alimentary canal, to profit from the breast and the milk it supplies. Put in another way, assuming alpha-function as that which makes available to the infant what would otherwise remain unavailable for any purpose other than evacuation as beta-elements, what are the *factors* of this function that relate directly to the mother's capacity for reverie?
>
> The mother's capacity for reverie is here considered as inseparable from the content for clearly one depends on the other. *If the feeding mother cannot allow reverie or if the reverie is allowed but is not associated with love for the child or its father this fact will be communicated to the infant even though incomprehensible to the infant.* Psychical quality will be imparted to the channels of communication, the links with the child. What happens will depend on the nature of these maternal psychical qualities and their impact on the psychical qualities of the infant, for the impact of the one upon the other is an emotional experience subject, from the point of view of the development of the couple and the individuals composing it, to transformation by alpha-function. The term reverie may be applied to almost any content. I wish to reserve it only for such content as is suffused with love or hate. Using it in this restricted sense *reverie is that state of mind which is open to the reception of any "objects" from the loved object and is therefore capable of reception of the infant's projective identifications whether they are felt by the infant to be good or bad. In short, reverie is a factor of the mother's alpha-function.*
>
> (Bion, 1962, pgs. 36–37 italics added)

Earlier in *Learning from Experience* Bion writes:

> To review the terms I have used so far: (1) the ego is a structure that, as Freud describes it, is a specialized development from the id having the function of establishing contact between psychic and external reality. (2) Alpha-function is the name given to an abstraction used by the analyst to describe a function, of which *he does not know the nature, until such time he feels in position to replace it by factors for which he feels he has obtained evidence in the course of the investigation in which he is employing alpha-function.* It corresponds to that function of a number of factors, including the function of the ego that transforms sense data into alpha-elements. Alpha-elements comprise visual images, auditory patterns,

olfactory patterns, and are suitable for employment in dream thoughts, unconscious waking thinking, dreams, contact-barrier, memory. Clinically the bizarre object which is suffused with superego characteristics comes nearest to providing a realization to correspond with the concept of beta-elements. But the concept of beta-element includes only sense-impressions, the sense-impression as if it were a part of the personality experiencing the sense. It is to be noted that the alpha-function may be regarded as a structure, a piece of mental apparatus producing the contact-barrier.

(pgs. 25–26, italic added)

From these ideas I would like to highlight the following:

1. The basic function of reverie is described as changing beta elements into alpha elements as a result of alpha function.
2. The alpha elements Bion describes are the ego functions of *perception* (eyes, ears, nose), usually turned toward the external world. *Yet these organs of perception usually have no modulating quality in themselves.*
3. Reverie is described as a something that needs to go on between mother and infant, but is a reconstruction from adult analysis.
4. Reverie is described as the mental equivalent of "digestion", and is the result of the mother's love, which consists of her ability to take in all feelings from the infant.
5. Reverie is considered part of the mother's *alpha function*, which remains an *abstraction* until its components can be understood.
6. Alpha function is sometimes considered a *function*, and at others as a *structure*. [1] *One way of viewing the differences in how reverie is viewed by post-Bionians is that some view it as a function, and some as a structure.*
7. At times, alpha function is considered as separate from the Ego, and at other times ego functions are considered part of alpha functioning.

In summary, in his use of the term reverie Bion was attempting to capture something essential in the psychoanalytic process and infant development. At the time, I don't think he could define it further than he did, nor do I think he was prone to define a concept for others, rather leaving it for them to define it for themselves. So we are left with a concept (i.e., reverie) that points to an event, which is *undefined while it is happening, that is part of an abstract process (i.e., alpha function) that may also be a structure. It has led to creative interpretations, as well as a plethora of meanings.* As it will become clear later, Bion didn't seem to think about reverie in discussing the clinical work of others, and his followers had their own views on reverie.

An earlier model

As the reader will see, the post-Bionians present their model as having turned the Freudian-Kleinian model upside down. Instead of trying to bring what is unconscious to consciousness, the Bionian model has now become one of making *the conscious more unconscious.* However, the Freudian-Kleinian model has always been about how to enrich conscious and preconscious experience by bringing it more in contact with what was unconscious. The post-Bionian model was previously outlined by Ernst Kris as early as 1936, when he introduced the term *regression in the service of the ego.* I will explore later how Kris described the ego's controlled regression into primary process thinking that leads to the creative process evident in the arts, but also all elements of life, including symbol formation both preconscious and unconscious. Later Ego Psychologists applied this to analysis.

As I think the reader will see, the concept of *regression in the service of the ego* could serve well as the basis for the analyst's reveries. I have privately wondered whether Bion's training as a Kleinian led to a tendency to disregard the burgeoning explanations coming from the Ego Psychologists. This critical view of Ego Psychology was characteristic of most of psychoanalysts in Europe and Latin America.

Note

1 A structure is an apparatus that exercises functions. So in Freud's theory, the Ego is a structure. A function is the work a structure does. From this perspective alpha function seems to be used by Bion as a structure with various functions, with reverie being one of them.

4

WAS BION A BIONIAN?

While it is difficult to find examples of Bion's descriptions of his psychoanalytic work with patients,[1] he did conduct clinical seminars in many places, some of which we have notes from or recordings. We also have a recently published discussion, by a former patient, of his work with Bion (de Mattos, 2016). These sources served as a basis for approaching the question that is the title of this chapter regarding the analyst's reveries. The answer to the question of Bion's clinical use of reverie is straightforward.

1. *There is no indication of Bion working with his or the analyst's reverie in any of the clinical seminars, or in his way of working as portrayed by de Mattos.*
2. In all his work Bion's emphasis is on what the patient is hiding. Bion understands that the patient is attempting to solve what feels like a desperate, frightening situation, but the words he uses to describe it emphasize an aggressive attempt to *fool* the analyst, the world, and himself. When reading of his comments in discussing cases, his method seemed closest to the Kleinian perspective at that time, with the focus mainly on *aggression in the transference,* with little evidence of interpretations of libidinal life. In fact, Ferro (Ferro and Nicoli, 2017) believed that "*clinically Bion was not worth very much compared to what he theorized*, in the sense he was a strictly orthodox Kleinian when he worked: this he had been taught, and this he did" (p. 66).

As I was searching for some glimpse of how Bion may have used his reveries, I was fascinated by how I saw him working clinically. The rest of this Chapter explores my impressions of his clinical approach, albeit from my own perspective.

The clinical seminars

Levine and Reed (2015) describe their view of Bion's clinical writings this way:

For all their brilliance, however, Bion's writings aimed more at the preparation of the mind of the analyst for his or her encounter with the patient and did not contain extensive clinical examples or specific recommendations for technique. His was what might be called a strategic/conceptual approach to understanding the analytic relationship.

(p. 449)

However, we do have Bion's thinking about clinical material in one of the 1967 Los Angeles Seminars (Aguayo and Malin, 2013), and the clinical seminars and supervisions he gave in Brazil in 1975 and 1978 (Bion, 1987). Although I will be focusing on these seminars, his Italian (Bion, 2005) seminars cover similar ground. In general, these seminars show what Levine and Reed (ibid.) suggest…i.e., he's mainly preparing the mind of the analyst. While it is advantageous to look at it this way, it might also be looked at as a possible glimpse into how he thinks about working in an analytic session.

While one needs to be cautious in viewing what an analyst teaches as synonymous with the way he might practice psychoanalysis, I have found certain consistencies in the manner Bion approached case material in these seminars that we might consider.

1. As noted above, *most strikingly there is no indication of Bion working with his or the analyst's reverie in any of these sessions.*
2. In most of his seminars Bion is focused on the question of character, and his suggested questions are about uncovering psychosis (Brazil) and criminality (Los Angeles).
3. As noted above Bion's emphasis in these seminars is on what the patient is hiding. Bion understands that the patient is attempting to solve what feels like a desperate, frightening situation, but the words he uses to describe it emphasize an aggressive attempt to *fool* the analyst, the world, and himself. His focus is mainly on *aggression in the transference.*
4. There are significant differences in how he responds to hearing the clinical material in these two different time periods. For example, in the Los Angeles Seminar he listens to the entirety of a lengthy process note, with only an occasional question. In the Brazilian Seminars, the presenter would give an initial description of the patient (i.e., it could be the patient's way of entering the office, his opening words, or a brief history), and Bion would begin questioning the presenter or suggesting what was unconscious. While it is impossible to know what Bion was thinking at the time, *I will explore this observation, and the next one, from the position that he may have had different ideas of what he wanted to communicate in these different seminars.*
5. In the Los Angeles Seminar, when asked what he might say to the patient, his responses seem at times like what one might expect from a mainstream Freudian, working within the Structural Model.[2] In the Brazil seminars, his method is consistently more confrontational, both with the presenters and what he imagines one might say to the patient.

It is important to remember in understanding Bion's views, especially of psychosis, that his model of the mind did not include Freud's move to the Structural Model or Second Topography (1923, 1933), and he remained focused on the major thrust of the papers on "the Unconscious" (Freud, 1915) and Freud's (1911) "Two Principles of Mental Functioning". In these papers, Freud focused on primary and secondary process thinking, with the view that unconscious thinking is equated with primary process thinking and that conscious thinking is the same as secondary process thinking. However, it is noteworthy that by the time Freud (1923) wrote *The Ego and the Id,* the concepts of primary and secondary processes all but disappeared. By 1933 Freud, after recognizing *unconscious parts of the Ego and Super-Ego,* finally concluded that the system *Ucs.* became more and more "to denote a *mental province rather than a quality of what is mental*" (p. 71, italics added). Thus, in Freud's new model there was the Id, Ego, and Super-Ego, any part of which could be unconscious. However, being unconscious was not necessarily associated with the kind of thinking that was previously labeled *primary process.* Freud's view of psychosis came to be associated with *structural deficits in the Ego,* which led to it being flooded with unconscious elements from the Id. For a Freudian, psychotic thinking would eventually emerge. Bion, on the other hand, was seemingly suspicious of secondary process thinking and seemed to look for its primary process roots.

The seminars in Brazil

I have chosen to start with these seminars as we have the added benefit that a case I felt demonstrated what was *characteristic of Bion's method in these seminars,* was also discussed by Ogden (2007b). Therefore, the reader will not only have my attempt to understand Bion's method, but also how Ogden and I understand it from our own perspectives. As you will see, I look at what Bion said in these seminars from two perspectives. The first is what Bion might have been trying to communicate *via the participants' experience of what he said.* Secondly, I take what Bion says as examples of his clinical technique, and discuss it from my perspective. Ogden emphasizes what he sees as Bion's attempt to help the seminar members *understand* a patient's denied psychotic state.

Clinical material

The presenter begins with a brief historical summary of a thirty-eight-year-old man, an economist, who had been in analysis for one year. He then mentions that this patient has some "ritualistic aspects" (Bion, 1987, p. 141). Bion asks about these behaviors that suggest ritual, and the presenter describes how the patient walks in mechanically, and always begins in the same way, "Very well, Doctor", and then uses certain expressions like "I have brought you some dreams today" (p. 141), or "I want to believe we will work well today" (p. 141).

Ogden and I react similarly when Bion immediately interjects, "Why does he say they are dreams?" (p. 142). Ogden (2007b) characterizes this as one of Bion's *odd* questions. In fact, in these seminars Bion will often hear a fragment of the beginning of a session, and immediately ask a question. It is rare for the presenter's material to proceed past these initial moments.

Bion continues:

> We do not ordinarily say to a stranger, "I had a dream". So why does the patient come to see a psychoanalyst and say he had a dream? I could imagine myself saying to a patient, "Where were you last night? What did you see?" If the patient told me he didn't see anything–he just went to bed–I would say, "Well I still want to know where you went and what you saw." If the patient said, "Ah, well, I had a dream", then I would still want to know why he says it was a dream.
>
> *(Bion, 1987, p. 142)*

After reading this I thought "Why wouldn't a patient start his analytic session by saying he had a dream?" since the patient is talking to his analyst, someone likely interested in dreams and not a stranger? In trying to understand why Bion would proceed this way, it seemed possible that he was attempting to get at the psychotic core defended against by the ritualistic behavior. One can see the possibility that Bion is emphasizing awareness of the unconscious, and that the analyst needs to avoid falling into assumptions that *keep firm boundaries between conscious and unconscious processes*. As Ogden (2007b) notes, "the patient is trying to convince the analyst that there is only one state—that of being awake—so that both patient and analyst can agree that the patient is not psychotic and is simply reporting what he perceives in a waking state" (pgs. 1197–1198).[3]

Another way to think of Bion's "odd" question is that he is not talking about the patient rather he is talking *to the group of analysts*. That is, he may have been challenging the group to re-think standard concepts to better understand the workings of the psychotic core in every patient. In some part of the psychotic psyche there is no difference between dreaming and waking states. Therefore, he challenges the group to wonder, "What is a dream?" "What is being awake?" In this way when a patient is in a psychotic state and says, "I had a dream" the analyst can hold in his mind the question, "Was this a dream or a delusion?"

My own reaction to reading what Bion said was a feeling of *dislocation*. I briefly wondered, "Who is the psychotic, Bion or the patient?" Would he really say these things to a patient? Therefore, my sense of what was real was jostled, mirroring the psychotic state and the analyst's mind in dealing with a psychotic core. In this I could see how Bion's method of teaching could be useful. On the other hand, I would find it hard to confirm the accuracy of his view (i.e., the patient is psychotic) without hearing anything further from the patient. It would seem the analyst would at least want to hear the music and words of the dream before knowing if it was a dream in the Bionian sense or not. Also, I would find Bion's active questioning of the patient as antithetical to the development of *reverie*, or seeing the defenses against them. It seems to me that the development of *reverie* would require allowing the *analyst* and patient to roam wherever their minds would take them.

What Bion presents as a model for the analyst is the analyst as detective, ferreting out ways the patient is attempting to avoid his unconscious, as if this itself was a pathological process rather than an inevitable reaction to the threat of the unconscious[4] (or a psychotic mind) becoming conscious. In short, as we shall see, it does not appear there is anything in Bion's approach with this case that would approach a post-Bionian view of the analyst's use of his reveries in working with a patient. One could suggest that it is the patient's psychosis, and the analyst's avoidance, that leads Bion to suggest working in this way. However, Bion's approach with this case is like his work with most of the cases presented to him in Brazil. It just might have been that Bion, working intuitively, sniffed out psychosis before many would have guessed at such a diagnosis. I certainly agree there is something in the patient's presentation that deserves analysis.

Ogden's understanding

Ogden, in responding to Bion's question to the presenter, "Why does he say they are dreams?" (Bion, 1987, p. 142) writes:

> Bion is immediately cutting to the core of what he believes to be the emotional problem with which the patient is unconsciously asking for help from the analyst: the non-psychotic aspect of the patient recognizes that the psychotic aspect of himself is dominating his personality and consequently he cannot dream. Bion is suggesting with his question that, to the extent that the patient is psychotic, he cannot differentiate dreaming from waking perception, i.e. he cannot tell whether he is asleep or awake. Consequently, the patient (to protect himself from this frightening awareness) pretends to be a person who is interested in dreams.
>
> *(Ogden, 2007b, p. 1197)*

In response to the questions Bion said he would ask of the patient (e.g., "Where were you last night?") Ogden responds,

> Bion, in this way, is saying to the non-psychotic part of the patient's personality that he understands that the patient does not know when he is awake and when he is asleep. So, when the patient tells him that he went to bed, Bion treats the 'dream' as an experience that has all the qualities of waking-life experience. Bion continues, 'If the patient said, "Ah, well, I had a dream", then I would want to know why he says it was a dream' (1987, p. 142). By not accepting the patient's use of the word 'dream' (which serves to evade the truth), Bion is helping the non-psychotic aspect of the patient's personality to think (which involves facing the reality of the current hegemony of the psychotic aspect of his personality). Bion is implicitly stating his belief that such recognition of the truth of what is occurring influences the balance of power between the psychotic and the non-psychotic aspects of the personality.
>
> *(Ogden, 2007b, p. 1198)*

In Ogden's view Bion's confrontation of the patient is necessary to help the un-psychotic part of the personality become conscious of the psychotic part. However, at the end of his discussion of Bion's method, Ogden reveals the following, "Though I greatly admire many of the qualities of Bion's analytic style that are brought to life in the 'Clinical seminars,' I do not view his style[5] as a model to emulate" (p. 1199). Ogden doesn't elaborate on the specifics of what he means, but leaves the reader with one of Bion's enigmatic statements, "'The way I do psychoanalysis is of no importance to anybody excepting myself, but it may give you some idea of how *you* do analysis, and that *is* important' (Bion, 1987, p. 224).

In my own view, it is hard to imagine how it would be helpful to confront a patient fearfully defending against his psychotic thinking with what he's most frightened of. Thus, I am doubtful of the wisdom Ogden suggests that "recognition of the truth influences the balance of power between the psychotic and the non-psychotic aspects of the personality" (2007b, p. 1198). To my mind an equally powerful truth for this patient, as presented by Ogden, is that he is terrified of knowing the truth (if it's true that he's psychotic). *These different approaches (i.e., interpreting directly what the patient is afraid of versus working though the defenses) have never been satisfactorily resolved in psychoanalytic thinking about technique* (Busch, 1999; Paniagua, 2001).

Bion's approach in the Brazilian seminars seems very different than a 1959 entry in Bion's *Cogitations* (1991), where he seems more aware of the need of the patient to understand an interpretation rather than being bombarded with questions.

> The task confronting the analyst is to bring intuition and reason to bear on an emotional experience between two people (of whom he is one) *in such a way that not only he but also the analysand gains an understanding…and does so through an appreciation of the evidence to which the analyst is drawing attention in the course of his interpretations.* It is not enough for the analyst to be convinced there is evidence for the truth of his interpretations; he must have enough evidence available to afford the analysand the opportunity of being persuaded, by his reason, of the cogency of the interpretation.
>
> *(p. 91, italics added)*

In fact, there are times when Bion's way of thinking seems more like what I described (Busch, 1993) as the analyst interpreting "in the neighborhood", a metaphor for an ego psychological approach to interpretation. In his paper on "Evidence" Bion (1976), after having a series of associations to a patient's image, wrote "I was still lost because I had no idea what I could say that would reveal an interpretation, *and would also be comprehensible to the patient*" (p. 313, italics added). In this Bion seems to be echoing Freud's (1910) warning in his paper on "Wild Psycho-Analysis", where he stated:

> If knowledge about the unconscious were as important for the patient as people inexperienced in psycho-analysis imagine, listening to lectures or reading books would be enough to cure him. Such measures, however, have

as much influence on the symptoms of nervous illness as a distribution of menu-cards in a time of famine has upon hunger…Since, however, psycho-analysis cannot dispense with giving this information, it lays down that this shall not be done before two conditions have been fulfilled. *First, the patient must, through preparation, himself have reached the neighborhood of what he has repressed*, and secondly, he must have formed a sufficient attachment (transference) to the physician for his emotional relationship to him to make a fresh flight impossible.

(pgs 225–226; italics added)

In this Freud is suggesting that the patient must be able to make some connection between what he is aware of thinking and saying, and the analyst's intervention. No matter how brilliant the analyst's reading of the unconscious, it is not useful data until it can be connected to something the patient can be pre-consciously aware of. Somewhere along the way Bion seemed to stray from this position.

Further thoughts about the Brazilian seminar

Returning to the Brazilian seminar, the presenter says the patient is an economist and then, seemingly associating, mentions that the patient takes his holidays before and after the presenter, and that the patient forgot to send a check for the previous appointments. Surprisingly, Bion wonders why the patient calls himself an economist, suggesting that economists should know about paying bills. He calls this a "peculiar state of affairs" (1987, p. 143).

The presenter had suggested to the patient that he was too worried about himself to remember his bill. The patient said he wasn't worried about himself, he was more worried about his wife and children. Bion points out how peculiar he thinks it is that the patient is talking about "facts", which we cannot do anything about and have nothing to do with what an analyst does. He goes on to say, "if there is nothing troubling him—and we know there isn't because he said so—then these 'facts' are nothing to do with us; we can't do anything about his wife and children, and we can do nothing about him because he is all right" (p. 143). Bion then suggests what he might say, "If what you say is right, I wonder why you have come to me. There must be some reason why you are spending time and money to come and see me. Can you tell me what you think I am, or what I do"? (p. 143).[6]

After reading this I again found myself thinking that Bion's approach was "odd". Just because someone is an economist, does that mean he doesn't have an unconscious that leads him to forget to pay his bill. Also, as the analyst attempts to empathize with the patient's worries about himself as the cause of his late bill paying, I was more impressed with how the patient couldn't allow the analyst's empathy to affect him. While Bion decries the patient's use of facts, and certainly we all know the deadening effect this defense can have, *he ends up treating what the patient is saying as a fact, rather than a reaction to the analyst's empathy.*

Summarizing Bion's method of working in the Brazilian seminars it seemed to me:

1. There is little evidence of discussions of reverie in Bion's approach to the clinical material.
2. Bion emphasizes in these seminars that the analyst shouldn't be fooled into thinking that a seemingly non-psychotic part of the patient is presenting what seems like a derivative of the unconscious (e.g., I had a dream), when it is likely the patient can't make the distinction between a dream and reality. Here he is making a sharper distinction than the post-Bionians who describe waking dreams (reveries) as part of everyday psychic life, and an important tool for the psychoanalyst in understanding what might not be able to be verbalized.
3. As is typical of his Kleinian thinking at the time, his primary emphasis is on *the patient trying to do something to the analyst* (e.g., convincing the analyst that he isn't psychotic).
4. His technique seems focused on *confronting* the patient on what he's attempting to do to the analyst or the analysis.
5. Bion's interactions with the presenters reminded me of parallel play in children, where two children are playing side by side but not interacting.[7]

The Los Angeles seminars

In these seminars, approximately ten years prior to the Brazil seminars, one gets the impression of a quieter, more contemplative Bion, most obviously seen in his being able to sit and listen to the analyst's report of the session without interruptions. However, I would like to highlight again that *Bion neither asks the presenting analyst about any reveries, nor does he report his own*. Striking once again is his emphasis on the aggression in the patient's material, while ignoring what seems like a sexual pre-occupation with anal intercourse. While such a preoccupation can mask an aggression element, it is important to make such a distinction since one cannot assume it is inevitably aggressive.

I will now review the clinical material and Bion's style in approaching it, and then report what he would say to the patient along with some thoughts he has via the analyst's stance in listening to the patient's material.

The patient presented was a successful businessman who had been in analysis one and one-half years. He came to analysis because of on-going depression, for which he smoked marijuana and took barbiturates. He described acting seductively with clients and female employees, and was thrilled when getting a strong reaction back, but guilty if the woman wanted to pursue it further. Most of the session was taken up with a dream, where there was criminal activity going on.

The dream begins with the patient in an alley, where he strikes up an acquaintance with someone who lived nearby, or this person's wife. The patient observed suspicious criminal activity going on in the alley. The man who lived nearby was a politician running for two state offices. The patient then saw a suspicious looking character lurking around. Next the patient reports that in the dream he and his wife returned to the alley where there were some black men who were noticing his wife in a threatening sexual way. He and his wife started running and found a store run by black women, whom he asked to call the police. He was confused as to whether he should wait for the police, or return to his car in the alley.

The patient associated to feeling depressed and anxious coming to analysis, and that he identified with the politician. The politician lived close to his people, but he was aloof from them. He then remembered that in the dream some police were there supervising demolition work, which surprised him, and said he enjoyed this unusual slum area.

The analyst told the patient that he looks at himself as the slum area, but there was also a grandiose side of himself who can run for two offices at the same time. The patient associated to anal fantasies (left undefined), which he had referred to previously without much detail. The analyst acknowledged to the seminar that colleagues suggested in the past that he tended to move away from these types of fantasies.

The patient associated to a talk with an analyst who told him of a patient who was a mess because he didn't have his anality analyzed, and then the patient mentioned the Rat Man and having similar fantasies of rats going up his anus. He went on to talk about doctors who end up disappointed in their wish to save people who are representative of themselves, and end up taking care of themselves by turning to drugs.

In his discussion of the case Bion focuses primarily on the patient splitting off the criminal side of himself, and attempting to fit in. While there is a refreshing directness in how Bion talks about his impressions of the patient, there is a harsh side also. Here is a summary of what he says.

Bion states that by going undetected in his life and work by "wearing a disguise" to fit in with his peers, the patient also gets away with all sorts of "delinquent activity and worse, whatever that worse is" even as he passes as respectable. Bion suggests this occurs in his analysis as well. In this regard Bion notes that the patient demonstrates "an essential hostility" to the presenter, to psychoanalysts in general and the analytic world at large. Bion says the patient believes the presenter and his psychoanalytic colleagues themselves constitute "a criminal class in which you can't be detected", this is, in which an inadequate analyst can hide out by passing as a competent analyst and that Mr. X's analysis is a "hideaway from life". Finally, Bion suggests that if Mr. X "mingles with the crowd, if he finds the right environment, he won't be noticed as being a delinquent person" (Aguayo and Malin, 2013, p. 116).

There seems to be general agreement with Bion amongst the participants in the seminar, and the analyst adds confirmatory data from the patient's past that included numerous adulterous affairs, and late night drinking of beer, masturbating, and eating special foods from his childhood.

Bion understands that behind the patient's behavior is a feeling of despair. He describes a "homemade analysis" by "making facts which explain why you feel as you feel" (p. 122).

> Get drunk. This explains why you see things, and why you have such odd ideas. You're just drunk, and everyone knows that's what happens to you when you're drunk. But if you hadn't gotten drunk, and you saw those same thing, that would be terrible.
>
> *(p. 122)*

Bion suggest that if you don't commit a crime the feelings of guilt would be awful, because there is nothing you can do about it.[8] However, if you do commit a crime then you can stop, "or you can take it along to an analyst, and get the analyst to analyse and so forth" (p. 122).

In Bion's analysis of the session the anal preoccupations from the patient's associations fade into the background. One could easily make the case that this dream is about the patient's conflict over anally penetrating a woman or man, and being penetrated. The criminal activity taking place in an alley might be a first reference to this topic, along with the black men in the alley who are making sexual remarks about the patient's wife (displacement), and first finding safety amongst black women, but then confused as to whether to stay or not. His fascination with this slum, and the politician running for two offices (i.e., orifices), also suggest his sexual preoccupation with anal intercourse as both the recipient and the doer.

Bion reports two things he might say to the patient, which surprisingly fit well within the Freudian model *of working through, based on analyzing the resistances* (Freud, 1914). Further, he analyzes resistance based on the underpinnings of Freud's (1926) second theory of anxiety (i.e., anxiety caused by a threat to the Ego), which I've noted is the central element in an ego psychological perspective, leading to the necessity to analyze the danger to the Ego (Busch, 1995, 1999, 2014). Here is Bion's approach:

> I would think the most promising approach to this would be to draw his attention to the fact that he is again telling me something which shows how well off he is. And at the same time, how frightened he is that his situation cannot be maintained.
>
> *(Aguayo and Malin, 2013, p. 125)*

In what I've described as an essential Ego psychological approach to resistances, we see how Bion first identifies the resistance[9] (i.e., showing how well off he is), and then how the patient is frightened and finally what he is frightened of.

At another time Bion interprets the patient's tendency to splitting by clarifying the way the defense is expressed, and then describing the underlying fear.

So, I think I would be inclined to say something of this kind. You were talking to me as if you were [a business manager]. Now what is more, we know that you've taken the precaution to get qualified as [a business manager]. So, the disguise is complete. But that's not what's troubling. What's troubling you here, is that I, or somebody, will realize that you aren't one.

(pgs. 126–127)

Bion goes on to explain how he wouldn't wait too long to point out the dread underlying the patient's split...i.e., his fear of psychosis.[10]

Specifically, regarding reverie, towards the end of the clinical discussion Bion describes how he approaches analysis. First, he talks about memory, and how he doesn't ruminate about getting the facts correct. Then after describing the special-ness of the analytic session, and quoting Darwin, "It's impossible to exercise observation and your judgment at the same time" (p. 130). Bion goes on to say,

Now unfortunately we've got to do it whether we like it or not. That's why I say that I think the actual interpretation one gives in a session can really be done almost asleep. Because by the time one is prepared to give them, one's got masses of information and so on, it's piling up, it's an accumulation of experience. But it must not interfere. One must be able to do it almost in your sleep. Because it must not interfere with taking in the information which is going to give you interpretations tomorrow, next month, next year, the next ten years if it comes to that. Otherwise you will not have it there when it comes to the point.

(p. 130)

There are two fascinating elements in this statement. The first is the necessity to take in what the patient is saying (i.e., the information), and the second is the analyst's state of mind while taking in this information. As we shall see when we turn to the post-Bio-nians, one often has the impression that *the patient's thoughts are getting lost while the analyst is lost in his own thoughts*. Bion seems to be suggesting that *we cannot get so totally immersed in our own mind that we forget the information the patient is presenting*. Further, I wonder what Bion means when he notes that the analyst can take in information and make interpretations in his sleep. The post-Bionians may take this state of sleep as akin to the waking-dream. However, Bion brings this sleep state up in the context of listening and taking in the patient's information. *Thus, I think Bion might have used this expression of "doing it in your sleep" in the colloquial sense...i.e., doing something without being aware one is doing it. This would fit with his view that one isn't trying to actively remember anything in the session, captured in the aphorism of working without memory or desire* (Bion, 1976).

An Analysis with Bion

José Américo Junqueira de Mattos (JAJM), a training analyst of the Brazilian Society left his country to undertake a brief analysis with Bion with many interruptions. The dates were from September 2, 1977 to November 10, 1977. It was continued in the month of May when Bion was in Brazil, and then in March and April 1979 when Bion was in London and on vacation in Saint Cyprien, France. It was then continued in London for the month of September 1979. In 1980 JAIM presented a paper to the Sao Paulo Psychoanalytic Society, "Impressions of my analysis with Dr. Bion", which was recently published in English (de Mattos, 2016, pgs. 5–22).

Apparently JAIM had other analyses, which didn't seem to be helpful in the way he felt he needed. From his account, it wasn't clear what he was seeking help for. He left his county fraught with uncertainties but with a feeling of hope that Dr. Bion could be of help to him.

Of course, there are many reasons for saying we can't tell anything about Bion's work from JAIM's account. First, we cannot tell if Bion thought of this as analysis, given the nature of the frame. Further, patients' retrospective accounts of their treatments are often colored by their own dynamics, even with sufficient attempts to analyze the transference. Further we have no idea of how Bion viewed JAIM's problems, and whether he felt he needed to work in a particular way because of that, along with the special circumstances of short periods of analysis interspersed with longer absences. Thus, all we can say is that this *may* have been the way Bion worked with this patient at this time in the context of an unusual analytic frame. Finally, as this is an account by a patient, we have no idea of where Bion's use of reverie played a role in his interpretations.

In presenting the story of his work with Bion, JAIM noted that, "Among my recollections I have chosen not only those that were important to me, but mainly those which I feel may be useful or even important to others" (p. 6). So, with all the cautions given above, I will treat JAIM's report as a *possible* picture of an analysis, and a questionable but potential way of understanding Bion's method of conducting analysis.

Impressions

For the most part Bion's method seems very familiar to many psychoanalysts…i.e., he listens carefully to JAIM's associations, and makes an interpretation based on JAIM's associations. While reading JAIM's account of Bion's responses I sometimes found myself thinking of something Bion said in the Los Angeles seminars, which expresses his passion for analytic work.

> And in the meantime, while I'm busy trying to remember what the patient says, I'm missing what's going on…even if you take it five times per week, how little one sees of one's patients! It's absolutely precious. The analytic session is so vital that one cannot exaggerate its importance, one needs to soak up every scrap of it.
>
> *(Aguayo and Malin, 2013, p. 130)*

At times Bion seems to stay close to what JAIM might preconsciously grasp in an emotionally deep manner. For example, during the first week of analysis JAIM is reminded of a poem he learned by heart at 13, which he repeats to Bion first in Portuguese and then English (which Bion requested). Bion then said something like, "As the poet looked for a reader who was able to read his book, you hope that I may also 'read' you what you can't read and know by yourself" (de Mattos, 2016, p. 7). At other times, maybe because of the unusual frame Bion and JAIM were working within, Bion tends to give more generic, symbolic interpretations that intellectually touch on what may be unconscious. For example, JAIM tells Bion of a trip he took to kill crocodiles. JAIM felt he rationalized this wish by telling himself he wanted to "tan their skin and eat their meat" (p. 13). He and his friend killed five amongst the hundreds they came upon, and he later felt depressed over the pleasure he received in killing. Bion commented, "Crocodiles are the remnants of the enormous pre-historical saurias and at present are the descendants of the first inhabitants of this planet. This impulse to kill you felt also had its roots in primitive man, whose remnants you still have within yourself when you feel pleasure in killing" (p. 13). This seemed like the kind of statement one might make to quiet a harsh super-ego, rather than analyzing its source. Most often Bion moves away from *why* the material reported by JAIM is coming up in the session *at that moment*, especially when there are potential transference implications. Again, I wondered if this had to do with the sporadic nature of the sessions with JAIM, and like in psychotherapy, one tries not to deepen the transference because of the limitations of the frame.

It is clear throughout the report of the treatment that JAIM had idealized Bion, and readily accepted interpretations even when he felt Bion was incorrect, with JAIM suggesting the interpretation turned out to be *incorrect in a positive way*. Given the tremendous sacrifices JAIM made to be in analysis with Bion, it would have been difficult for him *not to idealize Bion.* [11] At times when JAIM seemed able to allow himself some resistance to the analysis, Bion seemed to become frustrated.

> One day after several associations JAIM fell silent. Bion said that he saw no sense in what JAIM said, and asked him what he thought about it. After some reflection, apparently still in a resistant mode, JAIM said he thought nothing at all. Probably in response to Bion's comment JAIM said, "No doubt what I said was unimportant" Bion's response was the following, "If you think what you said is unimportant, why did you say it at all? Do you think that you are so rich that you can afford to waste time and money to come here and say futile, unimportant things?"
>
> *(p. 8)*

JAIM said, without describing any affective intonation, it was a remark he never forgot. [12] I can understand why. While Bion may well have been picking up on the unconscious hostility in JAIM's associations, the idea that this could be stopped with an injunction seems unlikely, while bypassing the meaning of what the patient was attempting to do. To be fair to Bion, it was a time when patients were often chided for being angry, or dismissive, as if it was enough to identify the negative feelings themselves. It was a time when interpretations according to the Topographical Model held firm. At other times Bion seemed to deflect JAIM's wish to *topple* him by lengthy, intellectualized associations. For example, after visiting Yosemite National Park, the home of the giant Sequoias, and talking of their beauty, JAIM "reflected that even the oldest and most powerful one day fall, die or are dethroned" (p. 11). He brought a postcard with a picture of the Sequoias and gave it to Bion. He states, "an inner pressure, which was so strong that I could not resist the impulse, had made me give him one" (p. 11). This is the kind of pressure we usually understand as an enactment of something that can't be put into words. After this bold enactment, he retreated to an idealized picture of his childhood that still conveyed he was talking about *power* (e.g., he remembered the *power*house near a water mill). JAIM also remembered a photograph of him at a young age "avidly biting into a juicy mango" (p. 11). Bion then said,

> "You suffer from the loss of your childhood. However, there is still another meaning. You suffer from the loss of your mother, the loss of her breast (these delicious mangoes), as you felt even at the time, did not belong to you alone, but to your father and to the brother that came before you and those that would come after you. One day you had to renounce this breast, this paradise, this welcoming ranch as one day you were also expelled from your mother's body. Here and now the same thing happens with me."
>
> *(pgs 11–12).*

Bion goes on to liken JAIM's feeling towards him with this wonderful ranch and mother that he will also lose. He goes on to interpret the postcard as how JAIM feels like this "Fallen Monarch who sadly returns to Brazil" (p. 12), being kicked out of paradise.

It is my impression that while Bion begins his interpretation along the lines of an Oedipal conflict; he switches mid-stream to the narcissistic loss of a grandiose self. It light of this lengthy, highly specific interpretation, JAIM writes on this same page, "Dr. Bion's comments and interpretations had the peculiar quality of never being *saturated*" (p. 12.) Yet throughout JAIM's account he mostly remembers what seem like highly saturated interpretations. It is difficult to know what he means when he describes this "peculiar quality". What seems peculiar to me is his describing Bion's interpretations as unsaturated.

At the end of his account of analysis with Bion, JAIM is modest about the impressions he reported.

> So, Dr Bion is not here among us to say what he would have said, and how he said it. I hope, however, that the impressions gathered here may not have undergone too many 'transformations', that the 'invariants' contained herein, in portraying the experience described, may be consistent with the lived experience.
>
> *(p. 21)*

As I stated in the introduction to the discussion of JAIM's report, one needs to be modest in coming to conclusions about it. Yet, if there is any accuracy to JAIM's remembering Bion's interpretations, they often seem consistently intellectualized, speaking to deeply unconscious parts of JAIM's psyche. Is this the type of interpretations that led Ferro to disparage Bion's clinical technique in comparison to his theoretical perspective? In reviewing the various reports of Bion's clinical statements, I came away with a mixed picture. At times, I had the impression that his way of working (i.e., working closer to the preconscious, defense analysis) fit with what I described (Busch, 2015) as common ground amongst seemingly diverse theoretical perspectives. At other times his approach seemed more intrusive, with a limited focus on what the patient was aggressively trying to do to the analyst.

Bion's limited reporting of his work with patients probably had to do with his centrality in the psychoanalytic communities where he worked and taught. Thus, most of his patients were other psychoanalyst, candidates, or those whose identity could not be easily disguised. However, as far as one can tell from these secondary sources, his understanding and the way he approaches interventions seems, as Ferro (Ferro and Nicoli, 2017) suggested, mostly influenced by Kleinian approaches. It was up to the post-Bionians to further the thinking on the analyst's reveries.

Notes

1 While I was doing a final edit of this book, a previously lost manuscript was published that included a brief discussion by Bion of a clinical case (Aguayo, Pistner de Cortinas and Regeczkey, 2018, pgs. 67–74). While it is a fascinating piece of history, his way of working with this very difficult patient only confirmed for me what I already wrote in this Chapter, and thus I will not discuss it.

2 In his review of these seminars Kernberg (2017) was very complimentary of the innovations Bion elaborated on (e.g., approaching each session without memory or desire, the need to accept not understanding, etc.).

3 This is based on Bion's view that the psychotic part of the personality is shown in denial of unconscious dreaming.

4 As viewed from Freud's later discovery of psychic danger being the cause of defenses (Freud, 1923, 1926, 1933).

5 In this same article, Ogden differentiates between analytic technique, which he defines as based upon a way of practicing developed by one's ancestry, and style based upon the analyst's personality and experiences, although he also views technique and style as inseparable.

6 There is more from this seminar, but I think this gives a good sense of Bion's thinking in these seminars.

7 "Although the child's activity is influenced by others around him, in parallel play there is no direct interaction between the child and other children" (Horner, Whiteside and Busch, 1976b, p. 462).

8 A similar point was made by Freud (1916) where he described "criminals from a sense of guilt" (p. 332)

9 In this I'm describing the resistance to the awareness of something frightening. Some might be inclined to call it a defense, which I would not disagree with. The distinction between these two terms in the clinical moment needs clarifying.

10 I think there is a danger in Bion's approach in that he is suggesting that the only reason for the patient's success is its defensive function. As we know, to be successful in any

field always includes more than just a defense, and to undermine his success may indeed lead to questioning all aspects of his reality and indeed lead to psychosis

11 As an example, he described how Bion always made what he thought was the right interpretation without fear of being wrong. He quotes Bion as saying, "I mean what I say and say what I mean", which JAIM attributed to Shakespeare. However, it had a familiar ring to me from a Dr. Seuss book *Horton the Elephant*, and also from Popeye (a comic book character).

12 It was my impression that after this remark by Bion, JAIM increasingly brought in more intellectualized material (e.g., paintings and books).

5

THREE POST-BIONIANS[1]

In reading the excellent collection of papers in Levine and Civitarese's (2016) book, *The W.R. Bion Tradition*, when it comes to the topic of reverie there doesn't seem to be a tradition. Basically, there are *many views* on *what is happening in the analyst's mind* that determine she is having a reverie, and the same holds true for what the *analyst might do with her reverie that is transformative for the patient*. In general, about the clinical use of reverie, *I would say that, at this point, there is no such thing as a unified post-Bionian view, only the views of post-Bionians*.

In general, while there is agreement amongst post-Bionians that the analyst's reverie is a co-construction of two minds in the analytic session, there are *different views regarding in what part of the analyst's mind a reverie is formed* (e.g., preconscious or unconscious), and sometimes a writer will change his view without noting this modification.

There is a broad spectrum of perspectives in the post-Bionian group, and I cannot do justice to all their different views on the analyst's reveries. Therefore, I have chosen three of the most prominent representatives: Thomas Ogden; Elias and Elizabeth da Rocha Barros; and Antonio Ferro. The main impression one draws from reading these authors is that there are both similarities and *differences amongst them in defining what is a reverie and how they use reverie as a clinical method*. Briefly, the da Rocha Barros and Ferro (for the most part[2]) see reveries occurring *in a specific form* (i.e., a dream like image), while Ogden thinks of reveries as an umbrella concept under which he includes a wide variety of psychic states that occur to the analyst in a specific state, akin to dreaming.

I will begin with the work of the da Rocha Barros as they, like *early* Ferro, define reverie as a *surprising dream-like image* that comes to the analyst's mind and contains strong emotional elements. Ferro uses the term *pictograms* and the da Rocha Barros call these images *affective pictograms*.

Elias da Rocha Barros (2000) defined the elements of reverie succinctly as an image "containing powerful expressive-evocative elements" (p. 1094). He goes on:

> I use the concept of *pictogram* specifically to refer to a very *early form of mental representation of emotional experiences,* the fruit of alpha function (Bion, 1963), that creates symbols by means of figurations for dream thought, as the foundation for and the first step towards thought processes.
>
> *(p. 1094, italics added)*

In short, da Rocha Barros presents the analyst's *affective pictograms* as an early form of thought, and the *first step* in a transformational process like one might approach analyzing a dream symbol.

Ferro makes a similar connection between what he calls the analyst's *pictograms,* and their potential for transformation of disturbing affects. Thus, he "postulates the centrality of the metabolizing activity we carry out on any and all sensorial and psychological impressions (via)…forming a visual *pictograph* or ideogram from every stimulus, in other words a poetic image that synchronizes the emotional result of each stimulus or set of stimuli" (Ferro, 2002b, p. 185, parenthesis added). However, on other occasions Ferro equates dreams (night dreams, daydreams) with reverie, *although there may not be an image involved,* and in his reveries *one finds reveries are not always equated with images.*

In short what the da Rocha Barros and Ferro (mostly) suggest is that *an emotionally charged image comes to the analyst's mind as a way of capturing a patient's unmetabolized affect,* and this image has the potential to transform a primitive feeling (beta element) into alpha elements. There are important differences between the da Rocha Barros and Ferro as to how this transformation occurs, which I will explore later in this Chapter.

Ogden's brilliance as a translator of Bion is unquestioned, along with his capacity for observing his internal states while reporting them unflinchingly. His ability to use what comes to his mind and the feeling states it leads to is a model for how an analyst can use his inner world to better understand his patients. His views obviously speak to many psychoanalysts as he is probably one of the most widely read and quoted authors of our time. However, in reviewing his work on the narrower field of the analyst's reveries, it soon becomes clear *how different his view of reveries is* from those of Ferro and the da Rocha Barros. In contrast to these authors Ogden (1997a, b) suggests that a certain slippage in using reverie is useful, and thus he considers a *variety of mental and physical states as reveries. These include: somatic states; memories; associations; and countertransference reactions.* As stated by Ogden reveries, "are our ruminations, daydreams, fantasies, bodily sensations, fleeting perceptions, images emerging from states of half-sleep (Frayn, 1987), tunes (Boyer, 1997) and phrases (Flannery, 1979) that run through our minds, and so on" (1997b, p. 568).

It is interesting that Ogden considers somatic states as reveries, given that they are typically viewed as devoid of representations. For example, Ferro (2016) views somatic states as "the evacuation of 'pure' beta elements that have not gone undergone incipient processes of mentalization or metabolization" (p. 196).

At times, Ogden views reveries as a state of mind in which the patient and analyst are, to a large degree, free to engage in an unimpeded stream of consciousness, "a type of consciousness generated by means of a relatively unencumbered interplay of the conscious and unconscious aspects of their two minds working/dreaming separately and together" (Ogden, 2012, p. 249). At other times Ogden (2007a, 2009) sees talking about plays, movies, or books in a way as "talking as dreaming" (Ogden, 2007a, p. 575).

Sometimes Ogden sees his reveries as preconscious, sometimes as coming from his own unconscious, and at others as an "unconscious experience co-created with the analysand" (Ogden, 2001). Birksted-Breen (2016) has suggested that Ogden's form of mental activity is not consistent with Bion's view of reverie. For example, Kernberg (2017) points out in his review of Bion's lectures in Los Angeles (Aguayo & Malin, 2013), *that Bion felt strongly that the analyst's countertransference is the result of his own unconscious*, while Ogden views it as inter-subjectively created within the patient–analyst pair.

On the technique of working with reverie

As I've noted above, it is always a difficult task to write about what one reads in the work of another clinician. It's basically a discussion of a *virtual* case, where I don't have the experience of being in the room with the patient to hear the music that goes along with the words, nor do I have a detailed history of the patient or the ins and outs of the psychic world of the patient and analyst. What I present is my understanding of the material from my perspective, which is basically Freudian. *I want to emphasize that I will be focusing in this book on how the analyst's thinks about and uses his reverie, and not the clinical wisdom that is also central to these authors' writings. In reading any one of them we come across creative ways of thinking that enrich our understanding of psychoanalytic treatment.*

Reflecting on the work of someone writing a paper and presenting clinical material is even more complicated, as the author has (usually) chosen this material to demonstrate a point in the strictest terms, one could say that all the reader can try to understand in the analyst's description is the work of the author with *this patient*, at this time, selected to demonstrate a point. Keeping this in mind, I've focused on choosing cases where the analyst's reverie is an essential element in the clinical material.

Elizabeth L. and Elias M. da Rocha Barros

I begin my discussion of the post-Bionian psychoanalysts with the da Rocha Barros, as I believe their understanding of reverie, and how it can best be used as part of a curative process in psychoanalysis, is most consistent with current views on the curative factors in psychoanalysis (Busch, 2014). Specifically, their work on reverie fits with contemporary ideas on the importance of building representations as part of the curative process. Thus, they use reveries as part of an interpretive process that focuses on the development of *symbolic thinking*. As I've noted earlier (Busch, 2014) there have been certain paradigm shifts based on an increased understanding of symbol formation as central to the curative process. Basic to this shift is the appreciation of a *developmental line of thinking that distinguishes symbolic thinking from more primitive levels of thinking (e.g., somatic reactions, language action, vague feeling states, etc.)*. As noted by Lecours (Lecours, 2007), what is represented can continue to build structure and enhance the ability to contain. This leads to what Green (1975) called, "binding the inchoate" (p. 9) and containing it, thus giving a container to the patient's content "and content to his container" (p. 7). In short, the da Rocha Barros present *a model for understanding reverie, and how it can best be used in clinical psychoanalysis, most consistent with current paradigms* (Busch, 2015). In what seems basic to psychoanalytic interpretive work, but turns out to be a departure from some other post-Bionians, the da Rocha Barros' view of how the analyst transforms his reverie into a useful intervention for the patient requires that "This symbolic visual form, within the process of building an interpretive comment for the patient, must be recaptured in the form of verbal symbols" (da Rocha Barros & da Rocha Barros, 2016, p.148).[3]

Elias da Rocha Barros (2000) introduced the term *affective pictograms* as an early form of mental representation that creates symbols via representations in dream thoughts, and is a *first step* toward thought processes.

> Strictly speaking, however, pictograms are not yet thought processes, since they are expressed in images rather than in verbal discourse and contain powerful expressive-evocative elements, and are different from beta elements, which are raw elements due to be expelled from the mental apparatus, when they are not transformed by the alpha function into alpha elements.
>
> *(p. 1094)*

Da Rocha Barros sees the analyst's reverie as only the first step towards the ability to think about an experience. According to the da Rocha Barros, *interpretations make emotional experiences available to thinking* via giving them symbolic form. As I will show later this becomes an important point that differentiates them from other post-Bionians, who sometimes see the *analyst having a reverie as transformative in itself*. I quote Elias da Rocha Barros at length as I believe he makes a central point that distinguishes his views from other post-Bionians as will become clear.

> *In my opinion, those who argue that the experience of dreaming is more important than its interpretation and that, as a result, interpretations can be dispensed with, are confusing two types of problems.* It is certainly true that the production of a dream represents a first step towards the ability to think of an experience. Part of the meaning of the experiences is already outlined in the dream work of transforming emotional contents that lead to the constitution of the pictographic images of the dream. Although the production of the dream is only the beginning of a process of emotional working through, it is a gigantic step

forward. In a primary stage, a dream maps out undigested feelings revolving around the more basic structures of the ego that constitute the kernels of meaning of emotional experience. These kernels of meaning are first apprehended in the form of pictographic images, which are a first step in the process of articulation of affects in the mind. I think that Meltzer has produced the best approach to this topic when he writes: 'The dreamer enlists the aid of the analyst to transform the evocative, the verbal language of the description of meaning, the first move towards abstraction and sophistication' (1984, p. 52).

(da Rocha Barros, 2000, p. 1098, italics added)

In his 2000 paper Elias da Rocha Barros ends with a quote from Fédida (1992, p. 16) that further captures his thinking:

When language is threatened by the domination of only what is visible, it can only free itself from this domination because words have the magic power of transforming one feeling into another, not just by some sort of correspondence, but by (emotional) resonance.

(da Rocha Barros, 2000, p. 1097)

In a joint paper, Elias and Elizabeth da Rocha Barros (2011) highlight the significance of *symbol formation* for thinking. "We start by stressing the idea that *the process itself of constructing the symbol in its different components and its vicissitudes is centrally important to contemporary psychoanalysis* since symbols are essential for thinking and for storing emotional experiences in our memory and for conveying our affects to others and making them explicit for ourselves" (p. 879). As they point out, we think and fantasize using symbols, and the symbolic transformations of unconscious fantasies allow meaning for our emotions.

They are particularly interested in a group of patients who have dreams, but seem unable to associate to their dreams except in the most concrete fashion.

They adhered to the analytic process, their dreams drew on quite many symbols, *but they were not able to recognize the full meaning of the emotional experience that appeared to be conveyed by the symbolic forms used in their dreams.* They seemed to have lost their ability to understand the *connotative* (subjective) aspect of the symbolic representations and only grasp its *denotative* (objective) side. The analogies involved in denotation became indications of concrete equality as in *symbolic equations.*

(p. 882)[4]

In a clinical example the da Rocha Barros (2011) describe a patient who has vivid dreams, but has no response to the analyst's interpretations of the symbolic meaning of the dreams. The patient reports that what the analyst says makes no sense to him, and doesn't understand how certain mechanical elements in the dream can stand for something else. The question the da Rocha Barros asks themselves seems obvious once they point it out, but hasn't ever been put so clearly.

We asked ourselves, what could be happening with this patient? On the one hand, he has some contact with his emotional experience that leads him to produce a dream comprised of sophisticated symbols. On the other hand, he appears not to have the slightest notion of the emotional experience that seems to be conveyed by the dream in his working throught process as we can see it taking place (or not taking place).

(p. 887)

In their discussion, they hypothesize it is an excess of intense emotion, like with a trauma, that leads to symbols losing their plasticity, and "silence the emotions, isolate the patient and thus cut off the patient from their meanings, as in this particular case that we are discussing" (p. 888). This leads to the da Rocha Barros' conceptualization of how they understood the use of *reverie with this patient*:

The analyst using *reverie* as part of the psychoanalytic function of his personality *begins* to occupy virtually the function of transforming the emotional experiences of the patient. In order to transform the patient's feelings projected into him, the analyst works with the feelings evoked in his mind by projective identification, either giving these feelings their first mental representation for non-mental states (*synthetic alpha function*, Caper, 2002), or changing the mental representation of unbearable mental states, so that the experience in the newly created representation becomes easier to assimilate by the mental apparatus (*analytic alpha function*). In both cases the analyst is broadening the connotative aspect of the emotional experience evoked in his mind.

(p. 889)

As noted above the da Rocha Barros understand a reverie in the analyst's mind as occurring in *affective pictograms*, something that exists between pure experience and a beginning abstraction of the experience. E. M. da Rocha Barros (2000) described pictograms astutely as an early form of mental representation of an emotional experience. They are not yet thoughts as they are expressed in visual images. *Using these affective pictograms as part of a process that leads to symbolic thinking is the unique contribution of the da Rocha Barros to current thinking on the use of reverie.*

As the analysis of the patient who couldn't dream his dreams progresses we see the emergence of previously split off emotions, and the beginning of the healing of the split. "At this stage, the analyst was basically *naming and connecting* the diverse experiences, dream images and feelings brought by the patient and, in so doing, propitiating a greater possibility of integration of different split-off parts of his personality through attributing meaning to what he was bringing to analysis" (p. 895, italics added). It is a strikingly different approach than how other post-Bionians work with reveries. Here the analyst is making links between previously disparate parts of the self, connecting feelings with images, and building representations like many other analysts might do.

Thomas Ogden

As noted earlier, over the last twenty years Ogden has been one of the most prolific and quoted psychoanalytic authors. It is easy to understand why after immersing oneself in his work. His theoretical papers are written clearly, often taking some of Bion's more obscure writings and making them understandable. His ability to capture his thoughts and feelings during an analytic session, and freely share these with his readers, is unmatched. His presentation of clinical material often reads like short stories. His erudition is obvious, both in the surprising references that pop up in his work, and the wide-ranging topics he has written about. However, reading his many clinical examples, one can see that *he not only has a different view of reverie than the de Rocha Barros and Ferro, but also a singular way of explaining the role of the analyst's reveries in the change process for the patient.* While Ogden's views of the analyst's use of his reveries *have been greeted as major breakthroughs, I don't believe their implications have been examined closely enough.*

Briefly the main differences between Ogden and the others include the following:

1. For Ogden reverie is an analytic *state* of mind, while the others view reverie as an analytic *function* that develops *spontaneously* at certain times in the form of an *image or affective pictograms*, not under the analyst's control.
2. Ogden considers psychic states like countertransference reactions or somatic reactions as reveries, while other post-Bionians do not.
3. Ogden has moved to the position *that it is enough for the psychoanalyst to have a reverie for a change process to occur in the patient.* In later years Ferro has sometimes come to the same position, while the de Rocha Barros have not.
4. In his associations (thoughts that come to mind rather than images), Ogden's musings are most often *lethic* ones (Schmidt-Hellerau, 2006), which can include excessive concern for others, along with thoughts about death, illness, guilt, etc. Some might also see this as a reaction to unconscious hostility, as Ogden often feels he has let someone down.
5. Ogden most often recognizes erotic transferences only retrospectively. However, they remain muted and often disappear from the session quickly.

Now for a more detailed examination of Ogden's ideas. He often describes feelings that are disturbing to him and seem closer to what Bion would have classified as beta elements (e.g., unpleasant somatic sensations, feelings of claustrophobia, etc.), along with associations that seem murderous...all of which he considers as reveries. In general, these beta affects seem the opposite of alpha elements, which are the beginning of the transformative process. *While recognizing these thoughts and feelings as countertransference reactions that cause him to be unable to think psychoanalytically, Ogden still considers them reveries.* One might think that it is the *awareness* of his intense countertransference reactions that helps Ogden to sometimes move toward a more benign listening stance, and the capacity to think, and therefore he considers these countertransference reactions as reveries. However, *it is the recognition of his disturbed state of mind, not the thoughts themselves* that may lead Ogden to a different frame of mind. Clinical experience tells us that it isn't just the recognition of a countertransference that changes the way we're able to think more fully about our patients, but this recognition is best combined with self-analysis of our contribution. This is the most difficult part of dealing with our participation in a countertransference reaction, and sometimes is put into relief by the idea that the patient put these feelings into us (projective identification).[5] Klein herself was cautious in the use of this term as captured in an anecdote from Hanna Segal about "a young analyst who told Klein he felt confused and therefore interpreted to his patient that the patient had projected confusion into him, to which Klein replied, "No, dear, you *are* confused" (Bott-Spillius, 1994, p. 352). Based upon *his* theoretical perspective Ogden (1997a) rarely seems to analyze *his* contribution to countertransference feelings or thoughts. As he states:

> I do not conceive of the analytic interaction in terms of the analyst's bringing pre-existing sensitivities to the analytic relationship that are "called into play" (like keys on a piano being struck) by the patient's projections or projective identifications. Rather, I conceive of the analytic process as involving the creation of *unconscious intersubjective events* that have never previously existed in the affective life of either analyst or analysand.
>
> *(p. 589, italics added)*

Thus, one often finds in Ogden's "reveries" thoughts about a *sick or dying friends*. Such thoughts might indicate to some analysts that it could be useful to consider hostile countertransference feelings. Given his perspective, Ogden's thoughts about these "reveries" don't go in this direction, but most often lead him to become more sympathetic to his patient. This raises the possibility that these thoughts are what Schmidt-Hellerau (2001, 2005, 2006) would think of as object preservative. However, there is a particular quality that accompanies Ogden's thoughts of sick and dying friends, and that is guilt, remorse, and in one case a temporary identification with a friend who has a heart attack. Such self-punitive thoughts usually suggest some unconscious sense of guilt over unacknowledged thoughts or feelings. It is interesting that Ogden seems more aware of hostile countertransference *feelings*, than possible hostile countertransference *thoughts*. I assume that since he considers these thoughts "reveries", by his definition they must be transformative and not destructive. Consequently, thoughts about remorse over dying friends are considered reveries in Ogden's way of thinking, and therefore cannot be hostile. In this way, Ogden's thinking can be quite concrete.

From another perspective, *at variance with much of the thinking in the analytic world, Ogden's view is that it is enough for the analyst to have a reverie, and not necessarily transform it into an interpretation at some point.* Ogden sometimes *dismisses the role of transforming the unmentalized into symbols and new structures, and its containing role.* At times the act of dreaming replaces interpretation. As he states:

it all starts with conscious lived experience that is rendered unconscious so that something can be done with it mentally by dreaming (unconscious thinking). Only at that point is the unconscious understanding of lived experience *some-times* made conscious by means of interpretation.

(*Ogden, 2017, p. 3, italics in original*)

He goes on to say, "I view dreaming as inherently therapeutic" (p. 3), and posits that one doesn't even have to remember a dream to serve the psychoanalytic function of self-understanding. He goes on to suggest *if one isn't changed by a dream then it isn't a dream.*

For Ogden, the analyst's reveries *themselves affect the analytic relationship and transform the patient's thinking.* Reveries just *are.* At times, it seems that for Ogden his capacity to have reveries becomes the sign of a healthy analytic stance, while the content is secondary. Further what he calls reveries many would call *associations.* If one considered them *associations* one might think they would be the beginning of a process, not an end, as Ogden views reveries.

In what follows I will take two clinical examples from Ogden's vast output to demonstrate his view of reverie, *along with how it translates into a specific clinical way of thinking that is different from his post-Bionian colleagues, and other theories about the curative process in analysis.* In addition, I will apply my Freudian perspective in thinking about these cases. I picked these cases from Ogden's vast oeuvre, as I believe they capture the essence of how Ogden views reverie.

As mentioned earlier, notably missing from Ogden's broad definition of reverie are attempts to understand the *dynamic meaning for him* of his reveries. Thus, where he sees reverie I think of countertransference feelings, defenses against them, resulting in changed feelings toward the patient, etc. I will look at Ogden's work on reverie from this dynamic perspective, as I believe it points to a potential pitfall of reverie as primarily transformational in itself. In a later chapter I will explain why I think the analyst's reveries require self-analysis as part of sorting out their meaning for the patient.

"Reverie and Interpretation" (1997a)

In this early paper on reverie Ogden (1997a) presents a patient (Ms. B) who seems to feel she gains power by feeling not well treated by her analyst.[6] There are various ways this may occur, but with this patient, Ogden experiences her silent complaints, and disdain for a variety of things including his interventions, with powerful countertransference reactions. One can easily empathize with Ogden, given what he experiences as a never-ending attack that seems to the patient like realistic complaints. From the very beginning of Ogden's description of the first reported hour, he is aware of several countertransference reactions to the patient, some of which are somatic (i.e., tensed stomach muscles, nausea), some are in a critical tone Ogden senses in his voice, and some are interpretations thought but not made. *However, Ogden considers these countertransference reactions as reveries, not as something to further analyze.* This is because Ogden believes,

> Paradoxically, as personal and private as our reveries feel to us, it is misleading to view them as "our" personal creations, since reverie is at the same time an aspect of a jointly (but asymmetrically) created unconscious intersubjective construction that I have termed "the intersubjective analytic third" [...] In conceptualizing reverie, as both an individual psychic event and a part of an unconscious intersubjective construction, I am relying on a dialectical conception of the analytic interaction. Analyst and analysand together contribute to and participate in an unconscious intersubjectivity.
>
> *(Ogden, 1997a, p. 569)*

The problem I see in Ogden's view is that if one elevates all one's thoughts to reverie, and reveries are considered something positive in themselves, *the distinct possibility we all know occurs where we have a countertransference reaction triggered by our own dynamics, is swept away.* Further, as I will go into detail in a later chapter, the view of analysis as entirely co-constructed, raises a variety of ethical (broadly defined) questions.

As with much of what Ogden writes, the problems with his views on reverie are mixed in with sound clinical advice, much of which I agree with. For example:

> The experience of reverie is rarely, if ever, "translatable" in a one-to-one fashion into an understanding of what is going on in the analytic relationship. The attempt to make immediate interpretive use of the affective or ideational content of our reveries usually leads to superficial interpretations in which manifest content is treated as interchangeable with latent content.
>
> Our use of our reveries requires tolerance of the experience of being adrift. The fact that the "current" of reverie is carrying us anywhere that is of any value at all to the analytic process is usually a retrospective discovery and is almost always unanticipated. The state of being adrift cannot be rushed to closure. We must be able to end a session with a sense that the analysis is at a pause, at best, a comma in a sentence. Analytic movement is better described as a "slouching towards" (Coltart [1986], borrowing from Yeats) rather than an "arriving at." This sort of movement is particularly important to be able to bear in one's handling of reverie. No single reverie or group of reveries should be overvalued by viewing the experience as a "royal road" to the leading unconscious transference–countertransference anxiety. Reveries must be allowed to accrue meaning without analyst or analysand feeling pressured to make immediate use of them. However urgent the situation may feel, it is important that the analytic pair (at least to some degree) maintain a sense that they have "time to waste," that there is no need to account for the "value" of each session, each week, or each month that they spend together.
>
> *(Ogden, 1997a, pgs. 569–570)*

Let me now return to Ogden's description of his work with Mrs. B.

My stomach muscles tensed and I experienced a faint sense of nausea as I heard the rapid footfalls of Ms. B racing up the stairs leading to my office. It seemed to me that she was desperate not to miss a second of her session. I had felt for some time that the quantity of minutes she spent with me had to substitute for all the ways in which she felt unable to be present while with me. Seconds later, I imagined the patient waiting in a state of chafing urgency to get to me. As she led the way from the waiting room into the consulting room, I could feel in my body the patient's drinking in of every detail of the hallway. I noticed several small flecks of paper from my writing pad on the carpet. I *knew* that the patient was taking them in and hoarding them "inside" of her to silently dissect mentally during and after the session. I felt in a very concrete way that those bits of paper were parts of me that were being taken hostage. (The "fantasies" that I am describing were at this point almost entirely physical sensations as opposed to verbal narratives.)

As Ms. B, a forty-one-year-old divorced architect, lay down on the couch, she arched her back, indicating in an unspoken way that the couch made her back ache. (In the course of the previous months she had complained on several occasions that my couch caused discomfort to her back.)[7] I said that she seemed to be beginning the hour by registering a protest about her feeling that I did not care enough about her to provide a comfortable place for her here. (Even as I was speaking these words, I could hear both the chilliness in my voice and the reflexive, canned nature of the interpretation. This was an accusation disguised as an interpretation—I was unintentionally telling Ms. B about my growing frustration, anger, and feelings of inadequacy in relation to our work together.) Ms. B responded to my comment by saying "that is the way the couch is." (There was a hardness to the fact that the patient said "is" rather than "feels.")

(*p. 572*)

Here Ogden views his several countertransference reactions, even his somatic symptoms, as reveries. Yet, as indicated in the work of the Paris Psychosomatic School, "somatic symptoms were the result of the inhibition or failures of psychic elaboration that proceed or accompany them" (Aisenstein, Smadja, 2010, p. 343). In short, they view psychosomatic symptoms as the result of a *problem in thinking, or non-thinking…*i.e., the failure of representation.

Continuing to think of his work with Ms. B, Ogden continually anticipates rejection of any interpretation he makes, or doesn't make. He then reports:

I began thinking about a scene from a film that I had seen the previous weekend. A corrupt official had been ordered by his Mafia boss to kill himself. The corrupt official parked his car on the shoulder of a busy highway and put a pistol to the side of his head. The car was then filmed from a distance across the highway. The driver's side window in an instant became a sheet of solid red, but did not shatter. The sound of the suicide was not the sound of a gunshot, but the sound of uninterrupted traffic. (These thoughts were quite unobtrusive and occupied only a few seconds.)

(*p. 575*)

While many analysts would wonder about the degree of rage we were feeling with such a thought, Ogden is uninterested in the *dynamic* significance of what he thinks. As he considers his thoughts as reveries, the dynamic meaning of why he had this image *now is* not of interest for him.

We next learn from Ogden that he then began having obsessional thoughts (he thought of it as a game but it didn't feel like a game to me) about the synchronization of a clock across the room, with the moment the digital clock on his answering machine next to his chair would change from one digit to the next. As we often learn that obsessional thoughts are a defense against murderous ones, it seems possible this was a defensive reaction against associating his memory of the corrupt official committing suicide with Mrs. B. and his anger at her. Seeing these thoughts as a "game" may suggest he was minimizing the odd nature of his thoughts.

In general Ogden seemed to be under the sway of beta elements as he describes a feeling at the time, which was a "disturbing nature of the claustrophobia and other poorly defined feelings that I was experiencing" (p. 576). Ogden then recalls a phone call from a friend earlier in the day, who tells him of his need for immediate bypass surgery. In what seems like a common guilt-laden reaction, Ogden has a fantasy of being told this same news, and imagines not waking up from the surgery. He interprets this as protecting himself by "narcissistically transforming the event in fantasy into a story about my receiving the news" (p. 586). If this fantasy was designed to protect himself, it seemed quite unsuccessful, as it is followed by a brief sense of numbness (dying), and intense fears of loneliness, loss, and never waking up. Ogden *hypothesizes, in retrospect,* that his feelings are a "reference to the oppressive 'living death' of the analysand as well as to my own anesthetized state in the analysis, from which I unconsciously feared I would never awake" (p. 586). However, at the time, Ogden's thoughts turned to another guilty reaction to a friend (J) dying of breast cancer, who he felt he couldn't be with to share her feelings of isolation. He describes the "painful feeling of shame regarding my sense that I had failed to appreciate the depth of isolation that J was experiencing" (p. 587). It seemed these feelings led to an important psychological shift in Ogden where he seems able to start to be in closer contact with his patient.

Ogden then reports:

> The symbolic and affective content of the reverie was barely conscious and did not yet constitute a conscious self-awareness of isolation about which I could speak to myself or from which I could speak to the patient. Nonetheless, despite the fact that a conscious, verbally symbolized understanding of the reverie experience did not take place at this moment, an important *unconscious* psychological movement did occur which, as will be seen, significantly shaped the subsequent events of the hour.
>
> *(p. 587)*

It is my impression that Ogden here moves from his murderous rage towards Ms. B to a reparation, ending in sympathy for Ms. B's plight. Is this the result of reverie, *or are the reveries a result of a defensive process that leads from murderous thoughts to sympathetic ones?* While it is difficult to give a definitive answer, the lack of consideration of the *dynamic meaning* of Ogden's thought is striking.

Ogden doesn't say anything in this first session, but Ms. B begins the next session with a dream.

> I was watching a man take care of a baby in an outdoor place of some sort that might have been a park. He seemed to be doing a good job of attending to it. He carried the baby over to a steep set of concrete stairs and lifted the baby as if there were a slide to place it on, but there was no slide. He let go of the baby and let it hurtle down the stairs. I could see the baby's neck break as it hit the top step, and I noticed that its head and neck became floppy. When the baby landed at the bottom of the steps, the man picked up its motionless body. I was surprised that the baby was not crying. It looked directly into my eyes and smiled in an eerie way.
>
> *(p. 578)*

It is tempting to think Ogden's shift in empathic contact during the end of the previous session may have helped Ms. B to dream. A subtle shift in how we look at the patient or say "goodbye" can have such an effect. Ogden, in contrast to his usual disconnected feeling from Ms. B's dreams, feels disturbed by this one, which he feels is a positive step (rather than feeling nothing). However, Ms. B didn't say anything else about the dream, and began a detailed account about a project at work, which Ogden saw as defensive. Ogden then makes a rare *emotionally saturated interpretation of the defense* by saying,

> I interrupted her after several minutes and said I thought that in telling me the dream, she had attempted to say something that she felt was important for me to hear and at the same time was afraid to have me hear it. Her burying the dream in the noise of the details of the project made it appear that she had said nothing of significance to me.
>
> *(pgs. 578–579)*

Thus, Ogden appreciates the importance of the dream, and recognizes the defense against it. What happens next is striking in that Ms. B, in an emotionally meaningful way, can insightfully observe herself and offer insights into the dream. Thus, it seems to me that when Ogden can appreciate the *meaningfulness* of something to Ms. B, and the defense against it, Ms. B is better able to become emotionally invested in *her* feelings and *her* ideas. She was upset at feeling "immobilized" in the dream, and felt she could see herself as both the baby and the man. Later, she says,

> she was very frightened by how easy it is for her to become the man and the baby in the dream, that is, how easily she enters a "robotic" mode in which

she is fully capable of destroying the analysis and her life. She was terrified by her capacity to deceive herself in the way that the man seemed to believe that he was placing a baby on a slide. She could easily destroy the analysis in this mindless way. She felt that she could not at all rely on her ability to distinguish real talk that is aimed at change from "pseudo-talk" that is designed to make me think she is saying something when she isn't. She said that even at that moment she couldn't tell the difference between what she really felt and what she was inventing.

(pgs. 578–579)

Again, there is a striking shift in Ms. B's capacity to self-reflect after Ogden recognizes *there is something meaningful to Ms. B in this dream, and her defense against it.* Recognizing defenses (resistances) is what Freud (1914) described as the first step in working though, the importance of which has been explored by myself (Busch, 1993, 1995, 2000, 2014) and others (Gray, 1994; Paniagua, 2001). It is a different way of working clinically than considering the analyst's reverie as the beginning of a transformative process for the patient.

From another perspective, Ms. B's first association to the dream was a sense that she often feels "dropped" by Ogden in the sessions, which she quickly *negated*. This negation seems to be a defense since what Ogden himself reports in the previous session is that he dropped contact with her via his countertransference reactions, and obsessional thinking. Further, while his reveries seem to eventually help him get back to the patient, I wonder how much the patient feels she is dropped at these times. It is worth wondering if the patient's thought about her own destructiveness is an internalization of her negated thought about the destructive effects of Ogden's disappearing.

The next session begins with Ogden seeing disdain when Ms. B picks a loose thread from the couch. *It is an interesting moment and raises the question of how we determine* what a patient is doing to protect herself, act out a fantasy, or when she is communicating a message. It turns out Ms. B had been in a cleaning frenzy since 4 a.m. She said she felt like a failure in life and analysis, and she felt there was nothing else she could do but control the "ridiculous things" she could. Ogden makes a general transference interpretation that this was an anxious response to her feeling she made a mess (i.e., saying too much) in the previous session, which the patient gives perfunctory notice of before continuing. It is hard to know if Ms. B's "perfunctory" response is a return to her disdainful feelings as described by Ogden, or a reaction to an interpretation that is off the mark.

Ogden then notices the light and shape on a vase in his office, which he associates to a woman's body. He then has an anxiety-provoking image of a stainless-steel container in a food processing plant, where the gears weren't working, and a catastrophe was about to ensue.

I was reminded of the extreme difficulty Ms. B's mother had had with breast-feeding. According to her mother, the patient bit the mother's nipples so hard that they became inflamed and breast-feeding was terminated.

I had the thought that I was experiencing a sensuous and sexual aliveness with Ms. B, but had been made anxious by it and had turned her femininity (her breasts) into something inhuman (the stainless-steel container and its nipple/gears). It seemed I was feeling that catastrophic breakdown would follow closely on the heels of sexual desire for, and sensual pleasure with Ms. B.

(pgs. 581–582)

In his phrasing, Ogden leaves it open as to who would have the catastrophic breakdown, and why this would be. What is interesting is that Ogden then reconsiders Ms. B's arching of her back in the first session, which he initially felt was a condemnation of his uncomfortable couch, as an "obscene caricature of sexual intercourse", although why it was "obscene" wasn't clear. I wondered who was feeling disdain towards whom at this point.

Ogden next reports that later in the session the patient remembers a dream she wanted to tell him, which she does in a lively fashion.

I've just had a baby and I'm looking at it in the bassinet. I don't see anything of me in its face, which is dark, heart-shaped, and Mediterranean. I don't recognize it as something that came out of me. I think, "How could I have given birth to such a thing." I pick it up and hold him and hold him and hold him, and he becomes a little boy with wild curly hair.

Ms. B said, "In telling you the dream, I was thinking of the fact that what comes out of me here doesn't feel like me. I don't take any pride in it or feel any connection with it."

(p. 581)

Ogden suggests to Ms. B that while she is disgusted by everything that comes out of her in the analysis, she felt frightened in letting him know of the love she felt for the child in the dream. The patient is appreciative of Ogden recognizing this side of her, but

at the same time, she felt increasingly tense with each word that I spoke, fearing that I would say something embarrassing to her. She added that it was as if I might undress her, and she would be naked on the couch. After another silence of almost a minute, she said that it was hard to tell me this but the thought had gone through her mind as she was imagining being naked on the couch that I would look at her breasts and find them to be too small.

(p. 582)

Rather than responding to the libidinal quality in Ms. B's lively way of telling the dream, and her sexual fantasy of being undressed by Ogden, his thoughts then go back to J, the woman who died of breast cancer. Ogden reports, "I thought of the agony surrounding J's surgery for breast cancer and became aware at this point in the hour that I was feeling both a wave of my deep love for J together with the sadness of the enormous void her death had left in my life" (p. 582). Turning Ms. B's libidinal thoughts into memories of destructiveness and loss allows Ogden "an experience of missing the humanness of Ms. B that I viscerally knew to exist, but was only being allowed to glimpse fleetingly from afar" (p. 583).

Ogden then interprets to Ms. B that "I thought her dream and our discussion of it also seemed to involve feelings of sadness that large parts of her life were being unnecessarily wasted, "thrown away." He continued in this vein. Ogden then reported that Ms. B had "tears on her face, but no sound of crying in her voice as she said that she had not previously put the feeling into words, but a good deal of her shame about her breasts is that they feel like boys' breasts that could never make milk for a baby" (p. 583).

One wonders if Ogden's desexualizing Ms. B's fantasy had a role in her depressive, regressive fantasy of the inadequacy of her breast to be attractive. Remember he turns Ms. B's conflicted fantasy of Ogden undressing her into an association about loss and destruction of the breast. Further we have Ogden's previous association to her breast, which seemed to create anxiety for him, leading him to turn thoughts of her breast to something mechanical.

Finally, in Ogden's description of his reactions in the work with Ms. B I often found myself perplexed as to how he came to his understanding of what was going on. For example, his *obsessional* thoughts about the two clocks in his office he describes as a *game*. He sees it as a "plea" (p. 588), and it is difficult to know how he came to this conclusion. Further it raises the interesting question of how we *know* something about our thoughts or feelings in a session.[8] In fact, his description of what the plea was about was equally puzzling as to how he came to this view.

> The "mental game" as I experienced it at this point was filled not with boredom, detachment, and claustrophobia, but with desperateness that felt like a plea. It was a plea for someone or something to rely on, some anchoring point that could be known and precisely located and would, if only for a moment, stay put. These were feelings that in the hour felt "multivalent," that is, they seemed simultaneously to have bearing on my feelings about J (not "old" feelings but feelings taking shape in the moment) and about the evolving analytic relationship.
>
> *(p. 588)*

As with our patients, it is often only when the analyst allows his mind to roam freely, to see what surprising thoughts come to mind, that gives a hint of the unconscious meaning in a game or a symptom. In Ogden's way of thinking it is only the first surprise (a reverie) that seems important, *not the surprises about the surprise.*

"On Not Being Able to Dream" (2003)

From the beginning of the session reported in this paper, Ogden seems to shut off knowing of the patient's dream while he pursues his own dream of what's occurring. Thus, he begins the description of a session in the following way:

When I went to meet Ms. C for our session, on opening the door to the waiting room, I was startled to find her standing only a foot or so in front of me. The effect was disconcerting: my face felt too close to hers. I reflexively averted my gaze.

Once Ms. C lay down on the couch, I began by saying to her that something unusual had just happened in the waiting room. She had probably noticed that I had been startled to find her standing closer to me than usual when I opened the waiting-room door. Ms. C did not respond to my implicit question as to whether she had noticed my surprise. Instead, she rather mechanically delivered what felt to me to be a series of pre-packaged analytic ideas: 'Perhaps I was sexualizing or perverting the event. Maybe I was angrily attempting to be "in your face"'. It seemed that these ideas were, for Ms. C, fully interchangeable. She went on to develop these 'thoughts' at length in a way that felt numbing.

(p. 24)

The beginning of this session raises a most interesting point. There are many moments in analysis when something unusual occurs as Ogden described. It can be something the patient or analyst does, or sudden loud noises coming from construction work next to the analyst's office, etc. While we can appreciate Ogden's startle response, it doesn't necessarily follow that the patient noticed it, or it might not have been the most important part of what happened for Ms. C. It seems possible this played a role in her packaged associations, as his response had a "packaged" transference feel. It is like those transference interpretations before an analyst's vacation that fits everything into the analyst's impending vacation. If one of our goals is to increase the capacity to dream, *don't we also have to respect the patient's defense against dreaming, and her right to have her own dream that we might not know about yet.* That is, before we interpret what *we think* the patient is thinking, we need to wait to hear what is on her mind *or appreciate her need to keep it hidden.*

Although Ms. C seems not invested in the incident at the door as Ogden experienced it, Ogden attempts to bring her back to it, with an interpretation based on his previous work with her. "In an effort to say something that felt to me less disconnected from feelings involved in the event as I had experienced it, I said to Ms. C that I thought she might have been afraid that I would not see her in the waiting room had she not positioned herself as she had" (p. 24). Ogden experienced these words as *vacant*, possibly because he still hadn't allowed Ms. C space in the session to know what *her* emotional response to any of this was, or even if she had any emotional responses to the door incident that are congruent with Ogden's. The problem, as I see it, is that *Ogden sees his feelings as co-constructed with Ms. B,* and thus doesn't feel the need to wait and listen for her to tell her side of the story. One might characterize this beginning derailment of the session in this way: Out of anxiety Ogden feels compelled to bring up a "packaged" observation on how Ms. C's entrance startled him, and Ms. C responds with a "packaged" response, which Ogden then responds to with a "packaged" interpretation.

Ogden then reports that Ms. C responded by recalling what he describes as "the inexhaustible minutiae" of her day. After saying that his interpretations to Ms. C often led to a barrage of empty words he reports, "It felt to me that, often, my need to interpret was motivated by a wish to assert the fact that I was present in the room. I was also at times aware retrospectively that my interpretations had been, in part, angry efforts to turn back on the patient her seemingly unending torrent of words and psychoanalytic formulations, which I found depleting and suffocating" (p. 24). So, it seems possible Ms. C's concreteness may be, in part, an unconscious compromise formation… i.e., both an attempt to ward off the hurtful feelings of Ogden's countertransference, and in another way, retaliation for his remarks expressed in *action language*.

Ms. C then recounts a restless night with several awakenings, and Ogden reports, "As was characteristic of her, she made no reference to her emotional response to any of the events she described" (p. 24). As we have seen before when he is annoyed, Ogden has a reverie about someone in a medical crisis, this time a former patient (Mr. N) who was in the hospital with a psychotic reaction to prescription narcotic medicine. Ogden then says, "This reverie about Mr. N left me feeling extremely anxious but the reasons for my unease were opaque to me" (p. 24). Ogden then talks of being in an extreme state that sounds like someone under the duress of unmetabolized beta elements, and what he calls a "countertransference psychosis" (p. 27). He is disoriented, loses track of time, and tries to orient himself by looking at the clock but the clock looks back at him blankly. He fears he is losing his mind. He later hypothesizes that his "psychosis" was due to "chronic reverie deprivation" (p. 27), which he likens to a psychosis that can develop after sleep deprivation.

How does Ogden conclude that his "psychosis" was due to "chronic reverie deprivation"? Ogden gives us no clue how this came about. I have found only one other reference to such a state (Hermon, 2016), so *psychosis due to chronic reverie deprivation* seems like an experience unique to Ogden. In his co-constructed world, the patient deserves some credit for Ogden's disturbed state of mind, but it's not clear how.

Ms. C then talks of selling her condominium and her annoyance with her real estate agent who wants the condominium to be "staged" (i.e., where an interior decorator arranges the condo for sale). Ogden thinks of various interpretations, but doesn't say anything because, "to have done so would have been to join the patient in the use of words to obscure my feeling of the arbitrariness of our happening to be in the same room—a room that did not feel like an analytic consulting room at that moment" (2003, p. 25).

Ogden tries to reorient himself to Ms. C by remembering why she came to treatment, which had to do with her feeling pointless in every area of her life. He remembered she tried anti-depressants, which led him to think of Mr. N again, and that he may have colluded with him in thinking his hallucination of Christmas music was only a reaction to the narcotic, and didn't consider *Mr. N was avoiding feelings of sadness*. Ogden tells us his *speculations* why this may have been, but then becomes aware of how rare it was in Ms. C's treatment for him to have a reverie. He feels relief in this recognition. I am struck once again by how he is able to get in contact with himself and the patient via feeling sorry for her, as he did in the previous case when he recognized the patient's loneliness.

The patient begins the next session with a dream. *As the reader will see Ogden is less interested in the symbolism of the dream than his own reveries.*

> 'I'm at a session with you. Ms. C pointed to the floor. It's here in this office in the morning, at this time. It's this session. Then it seemed to shift and I am in another part of a large office suite. There are lots of rooms, not just the ones that are really here. There was stuff all over the place. There were old yellowing plastic plates, empty paint cans—I can't remember what else—books and papers strewn all over the floor. It makes me anxious just to think of it. I couldn't tell what the room was used for. There were also paintings leaning against the wall five or six deep, but I could see only the back of the outside one. There is a desk drawer that I very badly want to open to see what's inside, but I woke up before I could open it. I was very disappointed that the dream was interrupted before I could look inside the drawer'.
>
> (p. 26)

Ms. C is silent for several minutes after the dream.[9] Ogden then has a reverie about a friend who died. *Thus, once again, friends or patients who are sick or dying are the subjects of his reveries.* The specific reverie he has at the moment is visiting his friend in the hospital, who was in a coma, and upon taking his hand being surprised how warm it was.

This leads Ogden to the following reflections:

> The reverie involving the unexpected warmth in E's hand contributed to my becoming consciously aware of the growing affection I had been feeling for Ms. C over the course of the past several weeks.[10] After a time, I said to Ms. C that I thought I had been off the mark in the previous session when I said that I thought that she had been worried that I would not notice her in the waiting room if she were not standing very close to me when I opened the door. I told her that I now thought that perhaps she simply had wanted to be close to me and I was sorry that I had not allowed myself to know that at the time. Ms. C cried. After a little while, she thanked me for having understood something that she herself had not known but which she nonetheless felt to be true. She added that it was rare for her to know something in this way without a million other things flying around in her head.
>
> (p. 27)

Ogden then feels "intensely sad" for Ms. C and all she had missed in living, and links it to what he had missed out in Ms. C's feelings of warmth towards him. He felt buoyed by the thought she still had many years to live and experience life, and associated this to Ms. C saying she was disappointed at the end of the dream, but she wasn't depressed. Rather she was excited about what she might dream "tonight".

It is fascinating that as Ogden feels better able to understand Ms. C over the next weeks, he hypothesizes that his previous inability to do so was caused by his "inability to dream Ms. C's emotional experience (her undreamt dream) which she had evacuated into me" (p. 28). *This is a description, not an explanation. An explanation would help us understand why he wasn't able to understand her evacuations better.* It seems if he uses her evacuation as an explanation it settles the matter in his mind, while the question of why he couldn't metabolize her evacuations is not pursued. Ogden experiences Ms. C as taking over his mind and holding it hostage, yet when he briefly experiences a connection to her via sadness in the first reported session, Ms. C can dream that night. Further, in contrast to what Ogden experiences as her numbing use of words, her dream is filled with numerous symbols that seem potentially meaningful if Ogden were interested in them. It makes me wonder who is preventing whom from dreaming.

In what seems like an eerie coda like what happened with the patient in the 1997 paper, Ogden feels a greater sympathy for Ms. C when conflicts over sexuality come to the fore. Ms. C had long been puzzled by why, around age twelve, she felt her father closed off what was previously a warm and loving relationship. Ogden and the patient now understand this as their mutual fright over the sexual and romantic feelings that were developing. Ogden ends his discussion still not quite owning his and the patient's sexual feelings in the transference when he says enigmatically, "These feelings and thoughts were used to do further psychological work with 'the waiting room incident': the patient and I became better able to dream (and thereby live) that experience together—an experience which kept changing as we kept dreaming it" (Ogden, 2003, p. 29).

Highlighted conclusions

1. Ogden's view is that it is enough for the analyst to have a reverie, and not necessarily transform it into an interpretation at some point. Ogden dismisses the role of transforming the *unmentalized into symbols* and new structures, and its containing role.
2. For Ogden, reverie is *the state of mind* he brings to the analytic session. He seems to see himself in a state of reverie even at those times when he has intense countertransference reactions, where he seems to lose contact with his thinking, dreaming mind.
3. Sometimes Ogden uses reverie interchangeably with countertransference, which seems not to be in the spirit of Bion's view of reverie, which is growth producing. He also equates reverie with free association, or sometimes just a lively conversation where the two are talking freely in a lively way.
4. Ogden considers all countertransference reactions as reveries. He doesn't make distinctions between hateful countertransferences, somatic countertransferences or positive ones.

5. While the goal of treatment is freedom to dream-talk, when Ogden does make interpretations they tend to be highly saturated, which tends to close off thinking. In fact, Ogden doesn't seem to be that interested in what the patient is communicating about his thinking. The few times he seems to genuinely appreciate something about what the patient feels, the patient has a dream.

6. He seems to have a continual problem with anger when patients are concrete. We may all feel this way at times. This can happen with Ogden in his very first session with a patient.

7. Many of the memories that come to Ogden's mind are of friends who have experienced misfortune, are sick or dying, whom he feels badly for, or for himself, or how he treated them. These often seem like hostile reactions directed toward the patient, with accompanying feelings of guilt, and at other times like defenses against these feelings. He doesn't think of defenses in his reactions.

8. Sexual feelings seem to be in the background of these sessions, but for the most part Ogden isn't aware of them, defends against them, or considers them secondary.

Antonio Ferro

Antonino Ferro has published extensively on reverie, and spoken on the topic all over the world. Those who have had the pleasure to hear him present are immediately appreciative of his warmth and the pleasure he takes in explaining his ideas. He is a master at clarifying complex processes with simple metaphors. I believe his concept of *unsaturated interpretations* is crucial for psychoanalysts from all theoretical persuasions. There are few analysts who are so expert as Ferro in weaving together a patient's associations. Yet, it is only in extensively reading his published work that we can glean *the new paradigm he is espousing for the role of reverie as part of the psychoanalytic curative process.* His view of reveries as a curative factor in itself is closer to Ogden's than the da Rocha Barros', but his views on what a *reverie is* come closer to the da Rocha Barros at some points, but not others. Furthermore, there are times when quoting Bion's views of the interpretive process Ferro sounds like other contemporary analysts who use their reveries[11] to listen to what is preconsciously available, and interpret to the preconscious (as noted in Busch, 2014). For example, Ferro (2006) notes, "sometimes certain interpretations have the same usefulness as somebody who launches himself into a lengthy explanation of the functioning of the digestive system to an infant" (p. 990), which is reminiscent of Freud (1910) suggestion that interpretations of unconscious meaning before a patient is ready, "have as much influence on the symptoms of nervous illness as a distribution of menu-cards in a time of famine has upon hunger ... (p. 225). Ferro has also stated, "to pull the rabbit from the hat, the ears must at least be visible or somehow perceivable" (2006, p. 990). Green (1974), some thirty years earlier, presented his own animal metaphor for the timing of interpretations when he said, the analyst cannot run like a hare when the patient moves like a tortoise. However, Ferro doesn't emphasize this aspect of his work (i.e., the importance of working with what is preconsciously available). It is also my impression that many of Ferro's interpretations could come from the analyst's "evenly suspended attention" (Freud, 1912, p.101). In his own words, though, Ferro (2006) sees his way of working as different than the classical concept of interpretation, that he characterizes as "replaced by the activities of the analyst, which activate transformations in the field, transformations which can also *derive from the changing of the analyst's mental state,* from minimal interventions that function almost as enzymes" (p. 991, italics added). Here we have Ferro's view, like Ogden, *that transformations occur via changes in the analyst's mind.* He states,

> What matters is how far the analyst's mind receives and transforms the patient's anxieties in the present; the extent to which the analyst's theory includes this is irrelevant. *The essential point is what the analyst does in reality from the standpoint of the micro-transformations occurring in the session, irrespective of what he thinks he is doing or of the dialect he thinks he is doing it in.*
>
> *(Ferro, 2002c, p. 9)*

In various clinical examples one gets the impression that Ferro believes that the analyst's ability to transform undigested elements even *after a session* can affect how the patient responds the following session.

> I shall here apply this Bionian principle (the patient as one's best colleague) to a dream, which I shall present as evidence that the α-function is constantly at work. A kind of satellite navigation system dreams in real time what takes place in the analyst's consulting room after an interpretation *need not in my view necessarily be interpreted, but it can be used to facilitate the development of the field.*
>
> *(Ferro, 2008, p. 199, italics added)*

In contrast, Ferro (2009) stated, "Central to the field is the analyst's reverie—i.e., his ability to make contact with his waking dream (and its constituents subunits) and to *narrate it in words*—thereby bringing about transformations of the field itself" (Ferro and Basile, 2009, p. 14, italics added). In fact, Ferro does a lot of interpretive work. His manner of interpretation is captured in this quote, "Bion also tells us that interpretation need not decode, but extend to a mythical narration, that is, to transpose into a script, narrative or filmic form, which actualizes and renders visible what is being said" (Ferro, 2006, pgs. 990–991). Therefore, it is difficult to pin-point how Ferro uses his reveries, as he vacillates between the importance of words to transform reveries and words as unnecessary. For the most part Ferro, in contrast to Ogden, differentiates between reveries and countertransference. Further, Ferro sees his movement to the use of "field theory"[12] as having reduced the significance of countertransference reactions in his work, except when the field is mute (e.g., negative therapeutic reactions, extreme silences, and impasses). As he sees it, "all the 'obscure' emotional events that used to be picked up by the countertransference are now *usually—before* activating countertransference manifestations—signaled by the field, provided that the analyst is able to listen to the narrations of the sessions as forming part the current field (Ferro, 2006, p. 1000). This seems to be part of why Ferro gives such weight to his reveries, as he believes they have been cleared of countertransference elements. It isn't clear how Ferro views the *form* of reveries. His stated view is that reveries take the form of pictograms. However, in the numerous clinical examples Ferro presents there are few reveries reported, and in his published book of reveries (Ferro, 2015), apart from any clinical examples, pictograms do not dominate. Here are some examples from his book of reveries:

1. "To write in the new city they covered whiteboards with a layer of black and slowly scraped away the colour to leave just slim black characters on the board which was gradually taken back to white. And they were satisfied" (Ferro, 2015, p. 105).
2. The end of the tunnel did not give onto the outside. There was a fresco on the blind rock depicting a landscape: all the cars smashed into it (p. 180).
3. He recorded every rattle of the long agony, every hiss, snort, or gurgle through to the long final silence. Whenever he worried that she might come back to bedevil his life as she had done for far too long, he put on the recording and rediscovered peace and serenity in the renewed confirmation that sweet music gave him of her death (p. 128).

Still, Ferro often presents his view that reveries are images. He sees pictograms, and their more primitive cousin, 'oneiric flashes',[13] as the basic building block whereby sensory impressions from all sources are turned into images that then can be turned into thoughts. Ferro believes reveries and *oneric* flashes are the way every sensory experience, exteroceptive and experience are pictographed[14] in real time. Further, Ferro believes it is the only way that pictograms formed from emotions are synthesized. "In reverie, *an image* that is usually thoroughly protected appears on the surface and can be seen with 'the mind's eye'; this is the maximum level of contact a mind can make with itself (p. 53, italics added). According to Ferro pictographs of alpha elements are unpredictable, but on each occasion represent a distinct creation akin to a piece of poetry or art. Like Ogden, Ferro views reverie as a means of accessing the waking dream thoughts that are going on all the time. "We can access this dream world in its continuous process of formation through our reverie in the analytic session" (Ferro 2002a, p. 598). *Ferro believes the analyst sharing his reveries is akin to self-disclosure, and only done in exceptional cases* (Ferro and Nicoli, 2017).

Ferro also postulates what he calls *narrative derivatives, which he equates with free association* (Ferro, 2015), as another method of shifting alpha elements into waking dreams. In contrast to Ogden, Ferro sees a difference between reveries and free associations in that reveries are characterized by a *direct contact* with the pictograms that are part of the waking dream. In contrast, narrative derivatives occur when the patient's use of free associations (in words) form an integrated whole, either as a development in the treatment, or in response to the analyst's interpretation. As he put it: "the sequence of pictograms (waking dream thoughts) is narrated—that is, put into words...*narrative derivatives* of the pictograms (or of the alpha elements, or of waking dream thoughts) are the outcome" (Civitarese and Ferro, 2013, p. 200).

Before turning to Ferro's clinical examples, I think it might be useful to highlight certain therapeutic principles he highlights:

1. "The ultimate goal of analysis is to enrich—or in some cases to supply for the first time—the equipment for metabolizing formerly unthinkable emotion and affective states" (Ferro, 2009, p. 178). He gives minimal importance to lifting repressions, insight, or making unconscious fantasies conscious, which seems to me to be part of building the equipment for metabolizing in the Freudian Model.

    a   Development of the alpha function and of the apparatus for dreaming dreams is the purpose of analysis. "Transformation into a dream is an activity carried on constantly by the analyst's mind, which strips the patient's communication of its reality status and regards the patient's narration as a dream that assembles, transforms and constructs itself in real time in the encounter between the two minds at work. This is so because the central operation performed in analysis is deemed to be enrichment of the *dreaming ensemble* (Grotstein, 2007)" (Ferro, 2008, p. 199).

    b   As in these sentences, Ferro is equating reveries with dream thoughts.

2. He uses dreams as a symbolic gestalt, while the *symbolic meanings of individual elements* are less important for him.

3. Ferro assumes when he has an image it is a reverie. From another perspective, it seems like it would be difficult to say *a priori* what an image represents.

4. When in a session, he doesn't think about the patient's history, childhood or sexuality.

5. He views the capacity for developing dream thoughts, in part, via identification with the analyst's way of functioning. "I expect that the patient will subliminally introject the mode of functioning of the field, even if I do not know very much about this mode of functioning" (Ferro, 2008, p. 200).

6. Ferro's *stated* view of transference interpretations can be easily understood by a heading in one of his books, "A disease called 'compulsive transference interpretation'" (Ferro, 2009, p. 171). However, what is striking is that in the few longer clinical examples published by Ferro, *his interpretations inevitably are transference focused.*

7. While Ferro has been the most articulate and convincing spokes-person for unsaturated interpretations, he has also said, "Needless to say, amongst the possibilities of intervention, which the analyst can use whenever it seems useful, remain the *saturated transference interpretations*, by which to make explicit the transference in the here and now (Ferro, 2006, p. 991, italics added).

8. Transformations from reveries occur via a process of *clarifications* (i.e., my (FB) term for abstracting the affective themes into terms available to the preconscious) followed by "possible contextualizations in the transference" (Ferro, 2009, p. 172).

9. It is my impression that Ferro's (Ferro and Nicoli, 2017) recent views have become more radical. As an example:

So, I believe that all of us…. have to defend ourselves from what we already know: all that is known should not interest us anymore. If we are convinced there is an unconscious, or something we call for now—I hope in the future it can be replaced by some other concept—and if we intend to concern ourselves with it, then it means it is the unknown that concerns us. All I know about a patient, once I know it, does not concern me anymore. My gaze, my attention, my ear should be directed towards all I do not know. The same is true regarding psychoanalytic theory: rather than enshrining it or making it an object of uncritical investment,[15] we should begin to set it aside.

(Ferro and Nicoli, 2017, p. 2)

As an example, Ferro suggests, "the concepts of transference and counter-transference were so important and have generated so many new thoughts and structures that by now we could easily do without them" (p. 2).

Francesco

It is not always easy to get a full picture of how Ferro works in that he mostly publishes short vignettes demonstrating various transformations that can occur with his method of working. However, he presents one example (Ferro and Basile, 2008) where he shares a reverie he has at the beginning of a session, and we can follow how the session proceeds. It raises an interesting question as to how the analyst determines if an image that comes to mind is a reverie or not.

I open the door to Francesco, a fine fellow aged about 30, and am for a moment disoriented when I see before me a tall, curly-haired, angelic-looking girl. I focus on the image and, a moment later, find my familiar Francesco again. Surprised and indeed utterly astonished at my sensory misperception, I impress on myself *that it must be a kind of reverie* but cannot find anything to connect it with.

In the previous day's session, I had given strong interpretations of aspects of sex life—or rather of fantasies linked to Francesco's sexuality, the patient having had one dream in which he was piloting an F14 and another in which he was the Formula One magnate Flavio Briatore at the controls of an off-shore racing craft. These images, although tending towards the manic, were indicative of new discoveries for Francesco, who had always seen himself as a respectful and sometimes deferential boy. He is in fact a very good boy, but as with anyone, that is not the whole story. The session continues with Francesco reporting a dream of a video game; then he comes to my consulting room, which is Room 360. I tell him that he seems to experience the analysis as a game, without forbidden angles or ones that cannot be explored—in other words, a 360-degree game.

With a surprised laugh, he says he is noticing lots of things that were inside him, which he did not know were there. He then tells me another dream: a male nurse with bad intentions goes up to a tender, delicate girl, perhaps wanting to attack her. Only then do I remember my initial reverie, of the nice, curly-haired girl, and am able to tell him that, perhaps, what I said about sexual fantasies yesterday, while on one level opening up hitherto inaccessible angles, on another had rather scandalized him. He fully concurs, saying that it isn't easy to discover oneself to be more like a Gérard Depardieu than one of the seven dwarfs as he had always thought. I answer that it is not impossible for even one of the seven dwarfs to have sexual fantasies about Snow White. He bursts into loud and liberating laughter.

(p. 9)

Again, I would like to focus here on how one determines the meaning of an image that comes to the analyst's mind. Thus, in this example Ferro assumes his initial image of Francesco as a "tall, curly-haired, angelic-looking girl", is a *reverie*. As reveries are assumed to be part of a transformational process of beta into alpha elements, what is being transformed with this image? We get no indication from Ferro. In my own understanding, after a session where Ferro "had given strong interpretations of aspects of sex life", and his phallic potency, Ferro's "reverie" turns him into an angelic girl. Is it possible that Francesco anticipated Ferro's response to his phallic strivings with the dream where this male nurse has bad intentions toward this tender, delicate girl? While Francesco views himself as emerging into Gérard Depardieu from one of the seven dwarfs, Ferro brings him back to being a dwarf, albeit with sexual feelings (i.e., it's not impossible for one of the seven dwarfs to have sexual feelings...).

From this example one might say that it is wise to consider an image that comes to the analyst's mind as a *potential* reverie, but not inherently evident that every image should be considered a reverie. It is my impression that it takes considerable self-analytic work to determine whether an image is a reverie in the Bionian sense, and this will be explored in depth later.

Lisa

Ferro (2005) describes a heroic treatment with Lisa, where she moves from being seriously disturbed, with fragile boundaries, that at times necessitated hospitalization, medications, and broadening of the frame, to finishing her studies, getting married, having a job, and two children by the tenth year of analysis. Ferro's admirably open and detailed presentation of what he did and what he struggled with in four widely spaced sessions raises many interesting questions regarding psychoanalytic technique, but I will focus on the session where he has an image and how he works with it.

In the session before the one reported Lisa talked about her shame over people finding out that she goes to psychoanalysis. Ferro's attempts to understand more about this leads Lisa to associate to an elementary school teacher who made her read things she didn't know how to read. Ferro, who feels he is by now familiar with Lisa's "persecutory" crescendos, leaves off further investigation on this topic. It was interesting to me that what seemed like a likely reference to how Lisa is experiencing Ferro's interpretations is bypassed, but when Lisa described her fear of neighbors seeing the mess in her house, he "interpreted this in the transference" (p. 1253).[16] She then talked about her husband who, seeing her undressed, commented, "What horrible big legs you have" (p. 1253). *Ferro then reports that the image of "an enormous gorilla appeared to me in reverie"* (p. 1253). The brief summary of the previous session stops there.

The complex question of what a reverie is can be seen in Ferro labeling his "enormous gorilla" image a reverie, which by definition is supposed to be the beginning of a transformative process. In non-Bionion language this would probably be called an association, possibly helping the analyst understand how the patent experienced her husband's remark. Birksted-Breen (2016) delineated reverie from other forms of thinking in the following manner:

> Reverie is also not the same as an image that might come to mind representing, as a metaphor, what is taking place. The single image I am referring to be closer to dream images than 'thoughts', and may seem quite unconnected with anything conscious occurring in the material...
>
> (p. 30)

Within this definition, the closeness of Ferro's image to Lisa's husband's remark would lead to further questions as to whether this was a reverie.

In Ferro's account the next session takes place on a Monday after Ferro cancelled the previous session. The patient comes in saying she was "bad", reporting panic attacks, wanting to run away, but being unable to move. With prompting the patient indicated *this wasn't about analysis*, but about her husband and being glad he was away and frightened he wasn't there. Ferro mirrors the patient's ambivalence, staying away from a transference interpretation for the moment. Lisa then talked about two movies she saw the previous evening, *King Kong* and *Krakatoa East of Java*,[17] saying one was in black and white.

> Ferro: It's as though in certain situations a volcano starts moving, or a gorilla, and you flee or remain paralyzed, in both cases terrorized. I have the impression that the volcano and gorilla correspond to a series of emotions that you haven't been able to 'read moment for moment' and that arriving all together they terrified you. I thought this was the meaning of your words in the last session about the elementary teacher who forced you to read things that you didn't know how to read, as I did in insisting on trying to get you to say why it was monstrous that someone knew that you were in analysis.
>
> (Ferro, 2005)

I wonder about Ferro's idea that in transformations of beta to alpha "what matters is how far the analyst's mind receives and transforms the patient's anxieties in the present" (Ferro, 2002c, p. 9) …i.e., *a silent process in the analyst's mind.* Further it is worth noting that after Ferro has the image of the gorilla the patient has a weekend filled with panic and feeling paralyzed. Unmetabolized beta elements seem to remain prominent. Ferro cancelling the previous session might likely have complicated Lisa's reaction. However, one might also think that *Ferro's gorilla image allowed Lisa to seek out the two movies that expressed her terror.* However, this is only my impression, as Ferro doesn't explain how the gorilla image was transformative.[18] Most striking to me was how Ferro's response to the movies was primarily an attempt to put the fears embodied in the movies into words. *In essence, providing symbols when there were none.* The session then continues:

> P: I have the impression now that you haven't spoken to me like this for a long time; I think you've understood me … that you are close to me.
>
> P: I also had three dreams: in the first I was on the motorway, going from one place, I had to reach another, but there were flyovers, crossroads, junctions; I couldn't understand anything any more—I was panicking; in the second dream, there was Angela, my maid, who had taken sheets covered in shit to the laundry; I was so ashamed; it wasn't possible; and then the laundry didn't clean them; they sent them back dirty; in the third dream, there was the countryside and they were cutting a tree down; it was the tree of life; it wasn't possible, it was excruciatingly painful and yet they were doing it, I was desperate.
>
> *(Ferro, 2005, pgs. 1253–1254)*

Ferro then asks Lisa what these dreams make her think of, and she replies, "Nothing. Once I knew how to interpret my dreams, lots of ideas came to me, now no longer; I don't know what to say … it's as though I had got lost in Rwanda[19]; I don't know which way to go (p. 1254).

What follows is that Ferro, using the dreams as metaphors, attempts to dream Lisa's dream for her, with varied success. It seems that Ferro felt, at that point, she primarily needed a "teacher" (i.e., the alpha function of the analyst). Yet, as noted above, the "teacher" in Lisa's associations was a shaming figure.

Can one see in this example how Ferro's image of the gorilla was transformative? Impressionistically one can see the possibility that the gorilla image might have led Lisa to watch the movies she watched, using them to express her fears. It also may have allowed her to have a dream and remember it. While beta elements infused her experience of the break and the dream, it may have been enough that this very disturbed woman was able to dream. However, ultimately, I find the connection between Ferro's image of the gorilla, and the subsequent session, vague and difficult to pin down. It is my sense that Ferro's use of an image, along with *his capacity to put Lisa's fears into words,* is what leads to her feeling closer to him, leading to her reporting a dream where she can show him what she fears most (i.e., what a mess she can make). Thus, one comes away with questions about Ferro's example regarding the importance of an image as a reverie. Was his gorilla image a reverie? What does it mean?[20] Is a reverie in the analyst's mind enough for a transformation to take place? Does Ferro attempt to change the under-metabolized into words more than he acknowledges? Reading through the many examples Ferro offers, it is my impression that transformations into words is a more important element in his analytic work than he acknowledges.

Filippo

The focus of this oft-cited paper, "The Patient as the Analyst's Best Colleague" (Ferro, 2008), is on how the patient's (Filippo) dreams (reveries) and narrative derivatives help the analyst understand the patient's reactions to the analyst's interpretations. As Ferro states,

> I shall here apply this Bionian principle (the patient as one's best colleague) to a dream which I shall present as evidence that the α-function is constantly at work. A kind of satellite navigation system dreams in real time what takes place in the analyst's consulting room after an interpretation. This dream need not in my view necessarily be interpreted, but it can be used to facilitate the development of the field.
>
> *(p. 199)*

Ferro also wants to highlight the concept of *transformation into a dream*, which he explains in the following way: "Transformation into a dream is an activity carried on constantly by the analyst's mind, which strips the patient's communication of its reality status and regards the patient's narration as a dream that assembles, transforms and constructs itself in real time in the encounter between the two minds at work" (p. 199). As noted earlier there are times Ferro (e.g., 2002c) talks about *dreaming* (day or night, words or images) *as a substitute for reverie, while defining reverie specifically as a pictogram.* Here we see him describing dreaming in the exact way he described reverie: "the expansion of dreaming in the waking state (the alpha function) is continually called upon to metabolize sensorial and perceptive debris (beta elements); the success or failure of this operation is always directly communicated by the patient, if one knows how to listen" (Ferro, 2002c, p. 480).

In his presentation of this clinical material (Ferro, 2008, pgs. 199–204), I was surprised by how familiar Ferro's method of working seemed *at times*. He takes Felippo's associations, and uses them for a transference interpretation like many analysts. When Felippo seems unaware of the transference feelings, Ferro turns to a more mirroring style, similarly to how a self-psychologist might ameliorate a defense.

There are further characteristics of Ferro's way of working with Felippo. He most often takes the patient's *preconscious thinking* and turns it into a dream like formulation. The patient's dream symbols seem of little interest for Ferro except when he (Ferro) dreams them. This fits with his Bionian view (Ferro, 2002b) that dreams function like Freud's Ego, in that conscious material needs to be dreamed to be psychically usable (for thinking, storing, etc.). As Ferro believes he made a harsh interpretation in the previous session with Felippo, he seems to be constantly looking for the *transference in the room*, even when it leads him to make further interpretations that seem *stereotypic and off* to him. His view on the significance of the field seems to be what prevents him from reflecting on his countertransference reactions. In contrast to Bion's view that the *analyst shall work without memory or desire, in this case Ferro works with both*. That is, he believed something was awry with his way of working in the previous session, and was primed to see the current session as the patient's response to it.

Ferro (2008) introduces the work with Filippo in the following manner,

> With a severely traumatized patient, I am at first not very interested in what happened to him and where and why; instead, I am concerned to put him back together, to sew him up, to support his vital functions, to oxygenate him and provide him with the necessary volume of fluids. My approach is to look forward rather than back...
>
> (p. 200)

He then tells us he wasn't happy with how he worked in the previous session, feeling that his comments could have been taken as criticisms, and out of tune. *[As in the previous case Ferro doesn't think of the patient's dream as having symbols with individual meaning that can primarily be understood via the patient's associations. Instead he takes the manifest content as part of the patient's psychic field, and treats it as a direct statement about the transference.]*

Filippo: I had a dream; or rather I had the same dream twice. There were aeroplanes, explosions, and a kind of bombing; and then some very long teeth appeared. They pierced through people, but didn't kill them. I managed to save my skin by hiding behind a solid wall.

Ferro: (*I think this is an accurate description of his view of yesterday's session and of my having interpreted with teeth, but prefer to avoid immediate saturation in that sense*): What does the dream suggest to you? (Ferro, 2008, p. 199)

The patient gives a vague response about emotions, and repeats how he could save his skin in the dream, while others were wounded, pierced by projectiles.

[Ferro's unsaturated intervention is one of his most important contributions in that it invites the patient to follow his own thoughts wherever they might go. In this way, we follow what part of an intervention, if any, a patient can reflect on. There is no point in the analyst directing the patient to an area of his dynamics if we don't know what is tolerable. Of course, there are times where a saturated intervention is necessary and important. What is interesting here is that Ferro's intervention has an unsaturated and saturated quality. When he asks, "What does the dream suggest to you?" he is asking an open-ended (unsaturated) question with the word, "suggest", yet given his thoughts on what the dream means he seems to search for the patient's reaction to the previous session (saturated). Otherwise, he could wait to see where the patient's thoughts go after he tells the dream.]

Ferro (2008) then reports he's unable to desist[21] from making what he calls a "rigid interpretation" (p. 201), "Was I perhaps a bit like a bomber who had you in his sights?" (p. 201). The patient denies this, citing what he felt was the "good climate" in the previous session. He then associates to two indigestible meals he had, one from his mother after the session and one later in the day at an ethnic restaurant. Ferro's response is the following: "(*I feel the need to offer an unsaturated interpretation so as to tone down the persecution; for me, it is a transference interpretation because I dream the characters summoned up there, in the field*" (p. 201)): So, on top of your mother's indigestible food there was the African cook's? You had a double ration of indigestible food.

[One might also see this, in part, as an unsaturated mirroring of what the patient just said, but the patient had mentioned going to an ethnic restaurant, and *it seemed the African cook was Ferro's dream. It isn't clear why an African cook was dreamt, and how it contributed to a transformative process.*]

The patient continued about his mother's awful food, and the cook's also, with all sorts of "rubbish" in it. If we follow Ferro's view that narrative derivatives help the analyst understand the patient's reactions to the analyst's interpretations, one might think this is Felippo's reaction to Ferro's interpretation, yet Ferro doesn't comment on it.

The patient then had a series of associations. First was of how his mother reminds him of a witch on TV who cuts off the flowers from roses, and put the thorny stems in a vase. Then he remembers a TV program from yesterday where a boy is taken out in a boat by his mother, and then abandoned, but he finds work as a chimney sweep. His thoughts then go to a movie he saw where a father and son lived like tramps but got by.

Ferro: All very upsetting, but hope won through in the end. (*But I can't resist adding another, superfluous comment*). I was also thinking that maybe I tended to bite yesterday. What I said was like sinking my teeth into you. I picked up on the thorns in what you said and emphasized only them, but threw away the flower, which is what I should have appreciated (p. 202).

[Here we see Ferro recognizing that he is countertransferentially pulled toward transference interpretations, but persists in this manner anyway, even after the patient is puzzled why Ferro keeps interpreting that he aggressively attacked him. While there is plenty of evidence for transference in the room at that moment (i.e., the patient experiencing Ferro's interpretations as "rubbish"). Ferro continues to focus on what he believes the transference *should be*.]

Felippo: Why do you say that?

Ferro: Well, I criticized your way of fitting in with the law professor's wishes (*which I had seen as a paranoid trait in the patient and criticized before owning and understanding the source of the persecution*), and above all when you mentioned the carpets and I stressed how you ought not to let yourself be trampled on (*I had wanted to interpret his way of bending to other people's wishes, but clumsily got the timing wrong*), instead of picking up the fact that you also wanted someone to teach you how to make a carpet yourself—to weave the thread into a fabric, and to organize threads of thought.

Felippo: Yes, what you said did surprise me.

Ferro: Perhaps my biting and then not saying anything triggered all sorts of feelings in you, from persecution to abandonment—being without a mother. You were left having to sweep all the soot from the chimney by yourself. But the main thing is that you got by even when being bombed and when you were left all alone: you managed in spite of all the difficulties.

[*This is a good example of how Ferro weaves together dream elements, and preconscious associations into dream-like interpretations, and leads to the patient's creative associations.*]

Felippo: And with his father's help, the boy in the film brought all his plans to fruition and learnt how to dream for himself.

Ferro: Let's hope the Eritrean or Sicilian cook (*the patient knows where I come from*) will not make any more indigestible food like that (p. 202).

While they both have a laugh at this point, Ferro in metaphor returns to his indigestible interpretations. The patient's associations go to the need to keep two views separate. Here I think he is trying to help the analyst to see there is a debate going on between them that only the patient recognizes preconsciously.

Felippo: (*after a short silence he goes on*): Yesterday my dad and my girlfriend's father had an argument about how to look after a vegetable garden. Martina's dad uses a rotovator, which is very fast. My father thinks it's better to use a hoe and do it by hand, partly because it goes deeper but mostly because, though the rotovator breaks up the surface better, its pounding ends up making the soil impermeable and preventing osmosis with the deeper layers. They decided to take one piece of the vegetable garden each, like the division into departments at the university: law on one side and economics on the other—each kept well apart.

Ferro: It sounds almost as if they need a barrier to keep the two areas separate (p. 203).

Here Ferro seems to narrate the patient's narrative in an unsaturated fashion, emphasizing the barrier rather than two separate ideas can exist side by side, and sometimes a barrier is needed. I think he tells the analyst why in his next association.

Felippo: Well, otherwise it ends like two cocks pecking at each other. I saw some cockfights in the Far East. They are exciting, but blood is shed and they go on pecking even though they are hurt. I'd rather play computer games. There is actually a cockfight game, but at least the blood isn't real.

Ferro: (I think he is drawing my attention to a risk: when I interpret too much and too automatically, this may superficially convey the feeling of a well tilled field, but can in fact make a deeper layer of the field impermeable, thus preventing even deeper levels from emerging. So, I refrain from making this interpretation, which I feel would be like decoding rather than the fruit of reverie). Ferro then says, "But perhaps law and economics could come to an arrangement, like the one between your father and Martina's" (p. 203).

[*Here is where, from my perspective, Ferro's emphasis on the field rather than unconscious symbolic meanings, takes the lead and, I believe, leads him astray. A barrier is needed between the two men because if there isn't, a cockfight might break out, with its possible homoerotic, phallic narcissism and fears of castration as a consequence. This is why a barrier is needed. Ferro, by raising the idea that the barrier may not be needed (i.e., perhaps law and economics could come to an arrangement), is suggesting these powerful fears the patient has about having a different view than Ferro are not that fearful (no barrier needed), when in the patient's mind they are very dangerous.]*

Felippo: Well, I realize that I'm also speaking about two conflicting attitudes inside myself: on the one hand experiencing emotions even if it makes me bleed because they are explosive, and on the other, cowering behind a wall like at the beginning of the dream, or in a video game (p. 203).

Here the patient speaks like a good Bionian patient, giving in rather than continuing the difference.

Ferro: But why do you think of the two attitudes in terms of either one or the other? There are some dishes, such as Sicilian caponata, in which salty and sweet flavors can coexist, like your mother's fiery nature and your father's excessive reserve in your own situation (p. 203).

(Again, Ferro isn't allowing in the dangers the patient feels he's facing, and preconsciously recognizes.)

In thinking about Ferro's work with Felippo, certain issues stand out. Ferro has a feeling that he was too aggressive in the previous session, rather than treating this as an idea he has had, and either waiting for what happens in the next session that might confirm or disconfirm this idea, or analyzing why he thought this, Ferro treats his feeling as *real*. It leads him to feel he *can't desist* from making transference interpretations, even when he realizes it's inadvisable. I believe this is a central problem when an analyst believes that whatever is going on is part of the *field*, as Ferro does. By denying the effects of the analyst's psyche, the need to reflect upon or test out our reactions is bypassed. Finally, by eschewing symbols for metaphors, analytic work loses a certain richness upon which it was founded.

In closing this Chapter I will end with a quote from Cassorla (2013), as I think he captures something that is sometimes missing in the work of some post-Bionians who follow the views of Ogden and Ferro. Cassorla believes in the subjectivity of each analyst, who must use his or her unique capacity to create images based on their *personal* experience (p. 206, italics added). He goes on to say that,

> Analysts must rely upon their intuition and develop their imagination, but the images which involve the analyst's capacity for reverie, must emerge spontaneously. In order to do this the analyst must bear the chaos and frustration of not knowing until something takes shape naturally. We are aware that in the face of not knowing, we seek to fill in for what is missing by including what we already know…The analyst must make an active effort to counter these tendencies. With practice, this active effort becomes automatic and connects Freud's fundamental rule of free floating attention to Bion's recommendation (1970) that the analyst should be "without memory, without desire, without intending to understand."
>
> *(Cassorla, 2013, p. 206)*

Notes

1 This was a challenging Chapter to write, and may very well prove the same for the reader. To show the important differences between the three post-Bionians, along with the paradigm changes inherent in how two of them view their reveries as part of the treatment process, I've had to use detailed process notes from their articles along with my comments about them. This close examination of process notes can be arduous to follow, but I believe it is central to grasping an analyst's way of understanding clinical material, and his view of the curative process.

2 I have added this proviso in that Ferro doesn't always limit his description of reverie to images.

3 A point also emphasized by Cassorla (2013).

4 The da Rocha Barros' view this as a result of the patient's attacking symbols in the process of their formation, and view it as a type of splitting. This raises an interesting question as to whether the process of creating and losing symbols might, *at times*, be more a defensive process rather than a destructive one. While they might boil down to the same result…i.e., the incapacity to symbolize…the different causes would bring about altered analytic approaches. For example, a defensive process would more likely lead the analyst to approach it from the side of the patient's fear (e.g., disorganization, loss, castration, etc.), while the destructive process might be interpreted as something the patient is doing to the analyst or the analysis.

5 While I find projective identification a useful concept, as a singular explanation for countertransference feelings I believe it to be too limiting.

6 What Schmidt-Hellerau (2008) described as the potency of a "lethic phallus". Or as moral sadism (2009).

7 In a session to be discussed later, Ogden considers that Ms. B's actions might be mimicking sexual intercourse.

8 This will be taken up in a later chapter.

9 This raises the interesting question, "How do we understand a patient who has a night dream, seemingly rich with symbols, but is unable to having waking dreams to her night dreams?" One could put it that the patient seems unable to represent her dream representations, or symbolize her symbols.

10 This observation seems surprising given his feelings earlier in the session.

11 In his reports, we mostly hear the result of Ferro's reveries, and not the reveries themselves. As noted earlier he has published a separate book on his reveries (Ferro, 2015).

12 Baranger, Baranger, and Mom (1983).

13 Oneiric is defined as being related to dreams. "Oneiric flashes", a term introduced by Meltzer reflects "an acquired capacity of the mind to face evacuative projective identifications, successfully organizing them into *oneiric* thoughts that cannot as yet find a sufficiently stable container. Consequently, they are indeed possible "dreams," but they are projected outward in isolated frames (Ferro, 1993, p. 391). "After years of absence there reappeared 'oneiric flash': 'I see a pair of pliers'" (p. 399).

14 This activity consists in forming a visual pictograph or ideogram from every stimulus, in other words a poetic image that synchronizes the emotional result of each stimulus or set of stimuli. This is called the alpha element. (Ferro, 2002b, p.185). As one can see this is a more sophisticated image than the oneiric flash.

15 While many may agree with Ferro's alternative to enshrining psychoanalytic theory, there are of course many alternatives to this or "making it an object of uncritical investment" (Ferro and Nicoli, 2017, p.2). For example, we can study it, learn from it, and apply what is still useful and explore the many aspects of psychoanalytic theory that are still unknown. See Busch and Schmidt-Hellerau (2004) for another perspective on theory.

16 This interpretation isn't reported.

17 A disaster movie from the late 1960s about an erupting volcano.

18 In this article, Ferro was only reporting clinical data.

19 Ferro explains, "Lisa calls her old way of functioning by the name of 'Europa', and her new way without drugs that exposes her to new violent emotive states that no longer belonged to her 'Rwanda'" (2005, p.1253).

20 For example, Schmidt-Hellerau (2005) points out "how King Kong, this huge gorilla is holding this tiny woman carefully in his big paw; he doesn't hurt her, yet everybody thinks he will and is afraid of him. Thus, while consciously feeling in the grip of a monstrous threat, she seems to preconsciously know and communicate that nothing bad will happen to her" (p. 1263).

21 Previously (Busch, 2014) I have noted that when the analyst feels compelled to say something it frequently means he is already in the midst of a countertransference.

6

FURTHER CONCEPTUAL PROBLEMS IN THE USE OF REVERIE

It seems to be the fate of new ideas about the psychoanalytic method that rather than being considered a valuable *addition* to psychoanalytic technique, they soon are considered a *replacement* for everything that has come before it. The case for a reverie-based treatment relying primarily on the analyst's reveries seems far from proven, and antithetical to how most analytic theories view the change process in psychoanalysis. While there are obviously good reasons for considering the analyst's reveries an important *addition* to the psychoanalyst's method of understanding, there are various conceptual problems that have important clinical implications that need to be sorted out.

Fifty years after Bion introduced his views on the analyst's reveries, trying to capture something that was more like an impressionist painting than a photograph, attempts to develop their clinical usefulness in the post-Bionian years have led to multiple, sometimes contradictory, views while their use by psychoanalytic clinicians has mushroomed. Bion captured something important in the re-introduction of this concept, focusing on the analyst's mind (in contrast to Breur and Freud focusing on the hysteric's mind), and he was wise in describing it as hard to define. Defining reverie sometimes seems like trying to capture the minute dust particles in a ray of sunshine through a dusty window. Its great appeal, I think, lies in the possibility it offers of understanding another's mind with a new method. However, *I find it worrisome when there is the wholesale use of a term while its definition remains different amongst its leading proponents. Further, I don't believe how it is used in the clinical situation by some post-Bionians has been carefully considered. Also, there doesn't seem to have been any acknowledgement of these differences to this point.*

In this Chapter I will sum up some of the conceptual problems in some post-Bionians' views of reverie, and their consequences. My focus will be on the tendency amongst psychoanalysts, in general, and post-Bionians in particular, to use a vague classification when greater specificity is called for. I will also suggest that various ways reveries are thought about that simplify a complex phenomenon.

The "Un" problem

Imagine trying to find a specific street in New York, but only being able to look at a map of the United States. The map doesn't give enough information to help you find what you're looking for. You can see that New York is on the east coast of the United States, but it won't help you find 1053 Fifth Avenue in Manhattan. This is one way of thinking about the "un" problem in psychoanalytic theory and technique. That is, when using global terms like the *unconscious*, we are referring to an area of the mind that has different qualities. In Freud's (1915) paper on "The Unconscious" he briefly conceives of *complex preconscious thinking with infusions of unconscious elements*. In a few sentences Freud, working within the topographical model, presents a view of preconscious thinking that goes from a permeable border of the system Ucs to the permeable border of the system Pcs. The deeper regions of the unconscious work differently and the characteristic of its content is unlike what is closer to the preconscious. Thus, when we talk about an unconscious fantasy it doesn't say very much without some greater detail as to where in the unconscious such a fantasy resides. Much as Freud described, "I find many of the examples of unconscious fantasies cited in the literature are more accurately described as preconscious thinking infused with unconscious elements" (Busch, 2006a, p. 1475).

While psychoanalysis, in general, has one "un" problem, post-Bionians have a number of "un" problems. As noted earlier, when the Bionians describe *unconscious* communications from patient to analyst, or an idea that is unconsciously co-constructed, there is little attempt to define where in the unconscious the unconscious communication is coming from and where in the unconscious it is received. Typical is a statement from Brown (2010), who describes a vignette where there "is a multi-layered intersubjective precipitate of the interaction between Billy's and my own unconscious communication" (p. 83). The post-Bionians have the added problem of a global meaning associated with the terms *un*represented and *un*mentalized. It is also hard to imagine anything in the mind that is *entirely unrepresented*. At the very least there would have to be some weakly represented state for it to be *recaptured by psychoanalysis*. Thus, it is likely there are a range of represented states from weak to strong. Further, as I have indicated earlier (Busch, 1995, 2009, 2014) memories and fantasies may be encoded in an earlier form of thought…i.e., action thoughts and language. This makes sense in that children have many experiences encoded in non-verbal forms so that they are represented, but not in words. Piaget (Piaget and Inhelder, 1959) tells us that up until ages five to seven, all thought is a matter of action in various degrees, with the action component diminishing as the child gets older. *Thus, thought is under the domination of action for a much longer period than has been generally recognized by psychoanalysis* (Busch, 2009, 2014). The reason for this "action" type of thinking has to do, in part with the way thought processes develop. As Piaget has shown, words and images are not the basis for thoughts. Action, encoded in sensory-motor schema is the foundation upon which representational thoughts develops. It is a primary mode of thinking through the

Oedipal phase. In areas of conflict when regression takes place, or with early trauma, the psychoanalytic clinician will most likely find action language as the primary form of representation. Loewald (1971, 1975) was one of the first psychoanalysts to note that words have a special power because of their roots in the *sensory-motor elements* of speech development.

Language action can have the same effect on the analyst, as what has been labeled as unrepresented thoughts, and we learn about it primarily through our countertransference. *However, how we work clinically will differ depending on whether we understand a patient's communications as language action or an example of weak thoughts. As language action is already a form of representation, it is easier to interpret using representational thought to build higher-level representations. With weakly represented experience, some form of representation needs to be built.*

Given all the above, it seems to me there is a wide range of levels of thought that are labeled as unmentalized and unrepresented rather than registered in a different form than words or images. For example, Ogden (2003) gives an example of a kind of talking a patient does about concrete events that leads him to experience "reverie deprivation" (p. 28), which he suggests can lead to psychosis.

> The patient agreed with what I said and without pause went on in a manner that was familiar to both of us, to tell me about the myriad events of her day. Ms. C spoke rapidly, jumping from topic to topic, each of which concerned a specific aspect of the 'organization of her life' (a term she and I used to refer to her operational thinking and behavior). She told me how long she had jogged that morning, whom she had met in the elevator of her apartment building on the way to and from the run, and so on. Early on, I had interpreted both the content and the process—so far as I thought I understood them—of such recountings of the seemingly inexhaustible minutiae of her life.
>
> *(p. 24)*

I think one has to be careful in labeling this recitation of concrete events as the result of the failure of representation rather than, for example, the patient attempting to *do* something to the analyst (e.g., rile him up, bore him) as a defense (for example) against an unconscious wish to have the analyst admire her in running clothes (i.e., a compromise formation).

Representations in other forms

There are forms of thinking in other modes of representation that can have the same effect on the analyst as reported by Ogden, but come from a different source than the inability to represent. For example, Oliner (2013) cites as an example the assumed lack of representation in, for example trauma, and what she describes as the "amazing accuracy of enactments and actualizations of calamitous events otherwise not available to consciousness" (p. 152–153). Oliner believes "it is impossible to think there is no link between the later event that gives rise to the repetition and the memory traces of the original experience" (p. 153). She considers the idea that there are *modes of representation* based upon developmental levels, rather than the issue of representation or its failure. This allows us to think about the continuity between the most primitive *modes of representation* and the most evolved. If we think of the goal of psychoanalysis as building more complex structures from a more primitive one,[1] it is useful to conceptualize different levels of representation akin to building a house. As I understand it the post-Bionian view is that on the site where a house is to be built there is nothing there, or at the other extreme there is a house. However, it is more fruitful, I believe, to think of different levels and types of representations. Thus, some form of thinking might be like a foundation for the house, others might be more like a foundation and the framework of the house etc.

False positives

If an analyst considers a countertransference sign or feeling as meaning only X, this can lead to multiple *false positives*…i.e., seeing a condition as existing when it is something else. It is my impression that this is a consistent conclusion for post-Bionions when an analyst feels distance from the patient, or a deadness in her mind, or reverie-deprived and similar states. The result can be that other possible meanings get shut out.

da Silva (2017) reports a week's sessions where there were some missing pieces in a jigsaw puzzle she and the patient (Joquim) put together.

> The week's sessions had passed with many oscillations and breaks in emotional contact. It seemed like something was disconnected, which was not the first time that I had experienced such feelings of countertransference. It was as if this analysis had various bands with nothing to link them together. Those missing jigsaw pieces also reminded me of a punctured container, and I soon associated with the traumatic situation Joaquim had experienced.[2] *I imagined those pieces to be the white spaces or blanks in representation, the trauma which was unpresentable.*
>
> (da Silva, 2017, pgs. 24–25, italics added)

It is when da Silva "imagines" the pieces as blank spaces in representation (i.e., unpresentable), there is an *assumption* that leads to the danger of false positives. Da Silva doesn't report Joaquin as being particularly disturbed by these blank spaces, and he is happy when the pieces are being put together, and when Silva fills in the blank pieces with paper. *In reporting Silva's work, I'm not suggesting she is incorrect in her assumptions,* rather I'm pointing to the possible problems when a concept or feeling state is *automatically* viewed as something specific like an unrepresented state, as it is amongst some current post-Bionians. It would be like a Freudian hearing a patient talk about a situation where there are three people, and assume that this is an unconscious representation of an Oedipal triangle. It is worth considering, but also important to listen for surprising meanings.

It seems to me there are many times when the analyst feels shut out from the patient's interior life leading to a feeling of distance or deadness in the analyst, that is the result of a distinct *dynamic* rather than a deficit in representation. For example, I (Busch, 2006b) have reported on my *role responsive countertransference* to the patient's defense, where I became disengaged from the work with the patient via feeling sleepy, lethargic, vague, leading me to interpret at a distance from the immediacy of the clinical moment. This seemed to be a reaction to the patient's unconscious attempts to dampen my enthusiasm for our work together. It only became clear over time that any excitement on my part in working with him led to fears of his becoming sexually aroused and getting an erection in the session, leading to feelings of narcissistic humiliation and shame. My role-responsive counter-transference was a response to his feeling of danger. There are multiple other moments where there is a *dynamic* explanation for the analyst feeling shut out. These include: the patient's unconscious identification with a cold, rejecting or depressed parent; the patient's projection of a silent destructiveness; the patient's need to be in a stage of haughty narcissism; the number of ways the analyst may withdraw from a patient's conflicts, and experience it as the result of the patient doing something.; etc. To confuse a problem of conflict with a structural deficit can be quite harmful to patients.

I think the *false positive* problem can also occur in considering *every* affective pictogram as a transformative reverie. For example, a colleague reported the following to me.

> M was speaking in her usual very low, monotonous tone of voice. This was her first session after my summer vacation, and I was getting reacquainted with how difficult it is to be with this patient. For a second I felt discouraged this was only the first session of the week and there were three more to go.
>
> She continued speaking, but I was not following her. Suddenly I had this image of a bunch of little adorable girls laughing aloud, from the bottom of their heart together, that lifted my spirit, I thought of my daughter at the kindergarten she has just started and her little friends laughing so hard when the teacher plays a particular song.
>
> My associations to the patient's history regarding laughing became immediately available. This is a patient that never laughs. There is a lifelessness to her sessions. She grew up with a mother who she is convinced was charging men for sex, while being married to her father. She would hear her mother laugh out loud with the men in the room. In the treatment any laughter, any sign of vitality, any joy, any elevation of the spirit is experienced as a disgusting sexual taboo.

In thinking about the image with the analyst, it became clear that it didn't add to the analyst's knowledge of the patient. The analyst knew of the patient's seeming joyless past, with the only laughter in her household associated with the fantasy (or reality) of the mother's laughter with lovers. The image seemed more a way for the analyst to revive her analytic mind, and once again find her libidinal investment in the patient. While one cannot rule out the possibility that the analyst was grasping the patient's own unconscious wish for herself, one cannot say for sure. The question remains whether this was a reverie of transformation for the analyst, patient, or both?

In my own psychoanalytic experience, I've worked with many patients like those described by Ogden (2007a). I'm specifically thinking of a patient, a woman, who was unable to establish long-term relations with men. She had no trouble attracting men, and would briefly become very interested in them, but this would soon fade. Early in analysis she talked non-stop. Further, a typical response she had to most things I said was to seem thoughtfully interested, but there was little evidence in her further thoughts that my words had any impact. Thus, it seemed that, not surprisingly, the developing enacted transference mirrored her relationship with men.

One day as she was talking I had an image of a sun-splashed scene, where a young woman, her hair flying behind her as she drove in a convertible along a beach road, wouldn't let me into traffic. It wasn't difficult to understand some parts of the image. While the patient was older than the woman in the dream, the sense I had of feeling I wasn't being allowed into her verbal traffic was conscious. Thus, I mused on why this image came to mind, and what it represented? My next thoughts went to a commercial from some years back for a *family mini-van*. In the commercial a middle-aged man is driving with his wife and children in the advertised min-van, when a young beautiful woman drives next to the mini-van in a convertible, and starts flirting with him before speeding off. The idea behind the commercial seemed to be to try and alleviate the anxieties of fleeting virility of middle age associated with driving a vanilla family mini-van. The message was you could drive this mini-van and still be sexy. This led to another memory of an old movie, *Get Shorty*, where through a series of funny circumstances, the family mini-van becomes the vehicle of choice for Hollywood actors and power brokers. Then a song came to mind, *California Dreamin'*, by the pop-rock group the "Mamas and the Papas". It reminded me of the year I spent in Southern California during my adolescence, where I thrived, and in my memory the sun was always shining, and my *mama and papa* seemed to be enjoying each other after a rocky period.

The following day two images suddenly appeared while I was listening to this patient. The first was of a young, hardy man who was walking in waist-deep water. It was quite a struggle, but he was making progress. The next image was the same, except it was an older, frail man in the same circumstances. This was followed by an association to an article I read the previous day where a fifty-five-year old man, an active adventurer who had survived many tests of endurance in extreme environments, died while crossing the Antarctic. While he was in excellent physical shape (the young man), in his last message he communicated that the effort of walking through deep snow caused him to lose his strength, with a feeling he couldn't go on (the old, frail man).

How to understand my *affective pictogram*? On the surface my first image added little to what I already understood about my patient's way of talking and my reaction. However, my associations pointed to an unconscious way I was experiencing my patient that I was unaware of. That is, I unconsciously seemed to experience my patient's non-stop way of talking as a challenge to my virility. At the time, I was aware of certain physical symptoms that made me mindful of my advancing age,[3] but I wasn't aware until this moment of how it might be affecting my response to my patients' resistances and character issues. The second image gave further evidence that my recent withdrawal into silence with this patient had a sullen quality, reflecting my wounded narcissism.

As a reminder, this example came to mind when I was considering the idea that *affective pictograms* were basically the result of the analyst's unconscious understanding of the patient, and the beginning of a transformative process. In this example the affective pictogram, and my associations to it, revealed an unconscious countertransference that was crucial to my understanding of how I experienced my patient's transference. From this perspective, the pictogram was extremely useful, but it shows the difficulty in seeing a pictogram as meaning only *one* thing. The affective pictograms were helpful to me in understanding an ongoing enacted countertransference. It only helped the patient after my working through my countertransference, and I could not say it was immediately transformative for the patient.

In short, I don't think we can say anything is any one thing in psychoanalysis. As I've tried to show in this section even affective pictograms, which I think have the most reverie potential, need considerable psychoanalytic work on the part of the analyst to untangle their meaning, and not fall into the category of a false positive.

Dreaming as understanding

In the post-Bionian view dreaming, and the capacity for reverie, are viewed as *super-alpha functions, and a basis for unconscious knowing*. For example, Ferro believes that "The aim of analysis is to develop the patient's ability to "dream"…and hence to transform, metabolize and therefore forget—the excesses of sensoriality and proto-emotions which, unless digested and "dreamed, lead to suffering and symptoms" (Ferro and Basile, 2009, p. 11). Ogden (2001) states, "I view dreaming as the most important psychoanalytic function of the mind: *where there is unconscious 'dream-work,' there is also unconscious 'understanding-work'* (Sandler, 1976, p. 40); *where there is an unconscious 'dreamer who dreams the dream'* (Grotstein, 2000, p. 5), *there is also an unconscious 'dreamer who understands the dream'* (p. 9) (Ogden, 2007a, p. 576, italics added). This view is challenged by patients who can't dream their dreams. That is, they dream but are *unable to represent their dream representations, or symbolize their symbols*. If the post-Bionian views of dreaming and reverie, as presented above, were accurate, one would expect a correlation between the ability to dream, and the capacity to dream one's dreams. It is also difficult to know how a post-Bionian would understand a patient presented by Aisenstein (2017) who had vivid daydreams but no night dreams. If nothing else the above suggests that dreaming is more complicated than a *transformative* event, or a royal road to unconscious knowing. Further, as the following example shows, there may be many meanings when a patient is unable to associate to his dreams, besides the failure of representation. This also raises the possibility that it is worth considering that when a patient isn't able to associate beyond concrete events in his life, other alternatives beyond the failure of representation need to be considered.

The patient who couldn't dream his dreams

This is an example of a patient that questions the idea that *where there is unconscious "dream-work", there is also unconscious "understanding-work"*. This patient could dream, but there seemed to be no *unconscious "understanding-work"*. Instead, his responses to his dream symbols were an enactment of a particular defense.

Mr. M began a session in the following manner. "So yesterday…I mean—there was all this feeling—but then it wasn't the same. I was relieved…. It was interesting…"[4] This was typical of Mr. M's way of talking, and I thought of it as a telegraphic, with lots of dots and dashes (like the old telegraph machines), and it often left me with no thoughts except a feeling of confusion. This was also a patient with frequent, extensive night dreams, filled with sexual symbols, but he was unable to have any associations to the symbols in his dreams. He mostly talked about how *he felt in the dream* or his *feelings about the dream*. Usually these were feelings of not being cared for. It is different than with a patient who feels embarrassed or guilty about the dream symbols. These patients will recognize the symbolic nature of their dreams, and approach them tentatively with meager associations. This patient's associations were to his feelings. A typical dream for this patient was the following:

> I was preparing to run a Marathon. I made sure my shoes fit just right so that my socks don't bunch up and cause blisters. I put Vaseline on my inner thighs so they don't chafe. I make sure my shorts aren't too tight so that they don't bind my testicles. This sometimes happens when I run. The marathon begins and I am running better than ever, leading everyone by a large margin. Suddenly I see a large snake in the middle of the road. I call over a race official who laughingly says, "no problem", takes an axe out of his supply box and gleefully chops up the snake. I'm horrified, but I begin to run again. However, my legs feel very heavy, I feel exhausted, and all the other runners start to pass me.

Mr. M's thoughts after reporting the dream were about how no one was around to help him, a familiar theme. While the transference implications about the castrating official were clear, transference interpretations at this point in the treatment usually went nowhere. Working in displacement I wondered if "his thoughts about no one helping were stimulated by the race official?". I thought this might lead us to the theme of castration, but all it did was to lead him to reiterate more about his feelings of not being helped, told in a telegraphic fashion. After this I was left with a feeling of agitation. At first I struggled to hold on to this feeling, and over time it seemed to me I was feeling interested in the sexual symbols, only to be told in action language by Mr. M that there is nothing to be interested or excited about. Over the next sessions I was reminded of a former patient whose husband was hooked on cocaine. The patient seemed to sense it, but couldn't be fully conscious about it. When we explored this she remembered a time from when she was about five, seeing her father drink some scotch first thing in the morning in a surreptitious manner, and when she asked, "Daddy, what are you doing?", he replied, "taking my medicine". So, like my ex-patient I was feeling with Mr. M that I was being told, "You think you're seeing something, but it's nothing".

Other session like this continued. One dream he told me had his family around a swimming pool, and I remembered hearing a paper years before where the analyst believed that swimming pool dreams were a reference to primal scene memories. One dream led me to have some further associations. In this dream he was in a room and next door there were lots of noises that sounded to him like fighting. I then remembered that early in the analysis he told me that until age six he slept in his parents' bedroom, and that when they moved to a larger house and he had his own room, he used to have to go past his parents' bedroom to go to the bathroom. His parents always left their bedroom door open. He remembered that for a period of time he tried to curtail his urge to urinate in the nighttime so he wouldn't have to pass his parents' bedroom. After this I remembered when my family's apartment was being renovated when I was about five, for a period of about a month my family stayed in a hotel, and we all slept in one room. This association came to mind in my analysis when I was trying to understand my frustration with instructors who I felt were saying things that didn't make sense. From these associations I could see that my agitation with M seemed, a countertransference reaction to something going on that I was listening to, but didn't understand. Both M's and my associations seemed to be a typical primal scene memory.

In a later session, Mr. M kept using the word "it", and I was unclear what the "it" referred to. I finally figured out the "it" Mr. M was referring to had to do with what he described as "our" understanding of a dream, which basically had to do with his *feelings* about the dream. However, my memory was that there was no understanding from the dream, only his feelings about the dream, and I had a "huh!" reaction in my own mind. He felt after the session that "it" (that word again) had come to such a *climax* and he could breathe again. Mr. M seemed to not have any awareness of the possible sexual meaning of this word. *My feeling was, there is something erotic going on here, but if I mentioned it M might acknowledge it, but not be able to do anything with it, like with the dream symbols.* Again, I felt agitated and wondered about my countertransference reaction…i.e., there is something going on that is sexual, but I'm supposed to not say anything about it.

I am generally cautious about making any interpretations based on my countertransference reactions as I try to sift through what might be more of my idiosyncratic reactions to a patient versus picking up something communicated, but not verbalized in my own mind, about the patient's communications. As Birksted-Breen (2012) said, psychoanalysis "requires a time of digestion and transformation, a 'reverberation time'" (p. 833). Once there was this confluence of associations to my countertransference I felt confident enough about my understanding of what was going on to begin the interpretive process. I began by making a series of clarifications (Busch, 2014) to see if Mr. M could grasp what I saw as the basis for my agitated state. For example, I would say to him, "I wonder if when you used the term 'climax' if its sexual meaning might have crossed your mind". Mr. M's response was that it did come to mind, but since he figured I would see that also there was no need for him to say it. This was how the enacted transference was expressed leading to my agitated feeling there is something sexual going on, *but we're pretending like there is nothing sexual going on*. Over time we could see how this was happening again and again when there were sexual references, leading to an understanding of how I was now in the position of the one experiencing the primal scene, left with the feeling of agitation and confusion as might be experienced by a young boy sleeping in his parents' bedroom. In my view there is no point in interpreting the underlying, until we have some agreement with the analysand on what is going on in the process (i.e., action language). In this way it is not like the post-Bionians who posit the need to build a beginning representation. *With language action the task is to change one type of representation (i.e., language action) into another form of representation (i.e., words).*

The model of reverie as the mother's state of mind vis à vis the infant

There are several ways to approach this issue. First there is little doubt that the mother's capacity to contain the infant's primitive emotions is central to their being transformed into something less toxic. However, research and psychoanalytic treatment since Bion's time makes it clear it is the thousands of ways the mother interacts with the infant (i.e., her attunement to the infant's feelings, the way she handles, talks to, feeds, baths, diapers, etc., etc. the infant), which effect how the infant will weather the storm of raw, unprocessed feelings and internal states. There isn't a direct correlation with how a mother dreams about the infant, and how she relates to him. One need only think of a mother along the more narcissistic range, who may dream of a loving bond with the infant, but gets irritated when the infant demands a great deal from her. Further, the development of alpha function is *not limited to infancy, but continues throughout the developmental stages of childhood*, and can be interfered with at any stage. One need only be reminded of the potentially regressive effects of separations around age two reported by Bowlby (Bowlby, Robertson, & Rosenbluth, 1952) to understand how the ability to modulate beta elements can be interfered with based upon life circumstances after infancy. Further, it is worthwhile to consider *there is no such thing as an effective mother who can modulate all feelings and fantasies*, but rather a mother who may be better or worse at transforming beta elements depending upon the child's developmental stage.

Some mothers can be excellent at soothing the storms of beta elements in infancy, but not so good at helping the child to modulate strong affects in the "terrible twos", when the child's need to be oppositional can be confused with hostility. Along the entire line from infancy to adolescence the manner of calming and symbolizing need to change according to the stage specific needs of a child, and a mother who is masterful in calming an infant, may not be so skilled when the child wants to separate or challenge her for the affection of the father. As Stern and Sander (1980) noted, the process of fitting or bonding involves two together unique dispositions and behavioral organizations that are highly disparate.[5] While Sander focused on the infancy until three years old, there is little doubt this *fitting together* goes on for a very long time.

One can think of the development of reverie in the mother–child dyad as involving (at least) *two distinct but interdependent functions*. The first is the mother's ability to contain and calm the child's upsurge of emotions. The second is the mother's ability to transform these emotions into *thinkable thoughts*. [6] Even with just these two functions the combinations of factors that lead to the capacity to dream are multitudinous. Let me present some examples that in broad guidelines give an indication of what I'm getting at.

An infant wakes up screaming. A mother can come into the room in various ways…i.e., calmly opening the door, soothingly talking to the infant while taking him into her arms. All the while the mother is talking to him in a calming voice…e.g., "mother is here now, and it's time to eat, but first we'll make you more comfortable by changing your diaper", etc.[7] Another mother can anxiously come into the room and bang the door open while rushing to frantically calm the screaming infant by picking her up and feeding her, but the mother's own anxiety leads her to hold the child in an awkward manner, and neither can get comfortable in the feeding process, while no words are spoken. Now imagine this scenario being repeated over hundreds of feedings, and then the child moves on to the next stage and similar processes are repeated. At this point we haven't considered the strength of the drives, the strength of the child's stimulus barrier, his temperament, etc. In these simplified examples, we get a hint of the multitude of factors leading to the capacity for reverie being enhanced or interfered with…and this is before the child has even understood a word.

All the above raises the question of the validity of Bion's metaphor of reverie as the core for the development of alpha function, and thus the basis for therapeutic change as seen in the work of Ogden and Ferro, where how one dreams the patient is enough for change to take place.

A different metaphor than the mother's reveries as the basis for psychic development

Analysts from and influenced by the French Psychosomatic School (Aisenstein and Smadja, 2010) have developed a different way of working with patients who appear like those described by the post-Bionians. Aulagnier's (1984) description of the mother–infant relationship presents an alternative to Bion's way of thinking how the mother's feelings translate soma into psyche. As summarized by Miller (2015):

> Meaning is conveyed and constructed through the quality of the shared bodily experiences within a topography implying the blurring of bodily boundaries... The mother's emotion, related to the manifestation of the infant's body will be perceived by the infant and it will inaugurate the *junction* between his psyche and the discourse and history that were waiting for him.
>
> *(Aulagnier 1984, p. 17 in Miller, 2015, p. 1366)*

While I also think this is a limited view, it does add another dimension to the mother–infant relationship.

The French way of working with more primitive patients who don't have the capacity for symbolic functioning is different than the post-Bionians. In an article that captures such an approach, Lecours (Lecours, 2007) argues that, "supportive interventions are the analyst's most relevant therapeutic means to help patients with feeble symbolic systems transform non-symbolic transference episodes and reestablish symbolic mental functioning" (p. 896). He follows Marty (1976) who pointed out that an *efficient preconscious* system is necessary for the building of a structural apparatus that allows for a greater capacity to contain. Without such capacity "conflicts are actualized into the 'real world' and call for an *interpersonal* reply" (p. 898, italics added). Thus, there is a tendency to enact the transference rather than reflect upon it. He believes that non-symbolic layers of the transference "can be worked through or transformed through a deliberate use of supportive techniques" (p. 897). While supportive measures often conjure up being kind or boosting up a patient's self-esteem, the French model is more sophisticated. An example from Aisenstein (2017) exemplifies this way of working in a consultation with a psychosomatic patient.

A patient is referred to her for consultation after he demands an operation for his sciatica from his rheumatologist as a "final solution" for his problem. The patient thinks the need for a consultation is ridiculous, suggesting he shouldn't have mentioned this term, "final solution" to what he believed to be his Jewish doctor. Aisenstein doesn't touch on the deeper meaning of this phrase but, after respecting the patient's silence, enquires into his profession, which has to do with movies. She then asked him if he was interested in dreams, which she described as "inner cinematography" (p. 15). The patient said he was, told four dreams, and then asked Aisenstein for her interpretation. She replied that she had none, explained why, but said she noticed a visual detail in all of the dreams...i.e., he was never standing. Aisenstein told him that in matters of the psyche one cannot reach quick conclusions, and told him something about the mechanisms of dreams, including that they are foremost the guardians of sleep. The patient recalled his powerful but disabled grandfather, the one man he had a vested interest in.

In this brief vignette, we see how Aisenstein doesn't touch on the deeper issues of the "final solution", and instead guides the patient to think about his mind and how it creates inner movies. When he tells his dreams, and challenges her to interpret them, she doesn't take the bait and explains why. She doesn't interpret the dream but clarifies[8] a theme to which he responds with an association.

Lecours (Lecours, 2007) argues that supportive interventions are the analyst's most relevant therapeutic means to helping patients with a feeble symbolic system transform non-symbolic transference episodes and reestablish symbolic mental functioning. He has a sophisticated view of supportive measures, different than the usual meaning of strengthening defenses.

> The expression 'supportive interventions' is used here in default of a better one that could encompass interventions addressing nonsymbolic contents and processes. Such interventions include any relational response by an analyst that emphasizes nonsymbolic curative elements.that are adapted to a nonsymbolic mental functioning. They actively provide to the patient a stimulus barrier, a container, a stimulant for creating mental representations, a support to the introjection of benevolent internal objects, a buffer against the projection of malevolent internal objects, the satisfaction of basic ego or self-needs, a validating mirror, etc. They allow for the ability to learn through experience when symbolic means cannot be used to deal with psychic suffering.
>
> (p. 908)

He presents a longer vignette in this paper demonstrating how he used supportive methods with a twenty-eight-year-old woman who recently made a suicide attempt. She experienced sexual abuse in early childhood, and currently is affectively overwhelmed by memories of the experience. Not surprisingly she soon experiences the analyst as abusive. Lecours focuses on a session where she felt forced by him to attend a support group for women who were sexually abused, where she experienced a female interviewer as cold and intrusive. Lecours doesn't attempt to interpret the ongoing enactment of being in an abusive relationship or the likely projection. For the reader, he highlights the patient's sense of conviction of the reality of her feelings and "underscores the obdurate concreteness of her transferential experience" (p. 903). It is my experience that when a patient is thinking this way, interpreting the underlying *meaning* of her feelings will, at best, make no sense to the patient, and is more likely for the patient to feel misunderstood. Instead, Lecours clarifies what he meant and acknowledges that he may have misjudged her readiness to participate in the group. He does suggest that she might have felt he was like her mother who was deaf to her objections. This is an intriguing intervention in that relating a current transference to past object relations is usually considered a deep interpretation. However, if a patient already verbalizes strong feelings about a parent, then connecting the patient's feelings towards the analyst to the past is likely more supportive than a new insight. Lecours' patient already knows she has strong angry feelings toward her mother, when Lecours makes the connection between her mother and the analyst he is building a new structure, where old feelings are expressed in the present as a beginning step in helping her work though her intrusive memories and the feelings they engender.

In short, the French model of the need for supportive measures in working with patients with primitive thought processes is different than the post-Bionian model.

Further, over the past forty years there have been significant advances in working with more disturbed patients that seem not to be included in reverie-based post-Bionian thinking about treatment. This is a vast area, and I will only mention Kernberg's recognition of the ego weakness in Borderline patients, the importance of applying Kohut's ideas of working with pathological narcissism, and the multitude of clinical suggestions exemplified by Steiner's (1994) "analyst-centered" approach. It is, as if, allegiance to Bionion thinking has led some post-Bionians to appear to be working in a bubble free from outside influences.

It is also worth noting that long before Bion, Freud (1915, 1923, 1926, 1933) and later the early Ego Psychologists explored how primitive thoughts and feelings were transmuted into structures and functions that helped buffet affects (e.g., Freud's 1915 paper on "The Unconscious" where he postulated how "thing presentations" were changed into "word presentations"). Freud's work on the Structural Model was followed by Hartmann's views (1939) on building representations, Jacobson's work (1954) regarding the ego's capacity to create mental representations of the self and the object, along with the first studies of the importance of the mother–child relationship by Spitz (1945, 1946), Bergman and Escalona (1949), Mahler (1968), Winnicott (1987), and many others. Further it is worth reminding ourselves that decades before Bion, Kris (1936) described what he called *regression in the service of the ego*, whereby a controlled regression takes place that allows for the integration of primitive thoughts and affects. While Kris's focus was on the creative process, and a patient's capacity to go onto a state very much like reverie, he also described its importance in the analyst's use of his own mind.

> The possibility suggests itself that a considerable tension between the regression in the analytic situation, and its more or less smooth control may characterize some of those rare individuals who show what one loosely calls a gift for analytic work, or at least a gift for it in an important respect.
>
> *(p. 266)*

By mentioning these developments before the evolving of Bion's theory, I want to just note the tendency in psychoanalysis for one theory to isolate itself from others, which has persisted to this time, and has resulted in a fragmented theory of the mind and psychoanalytic technique.

Lack of clarity and consistency in the definition of reverie

In evaluating the usefulness of any psychoanalytic concept there should be a certain *reliability*[9] or *stability* of meaning amongst those using the term. This is basic to the development of any construct across fields of study. At its simplest level, it can only lead to confusion if we think the post-Bionian we are reading or listening to has one definition of reverie, but in reality the author has his own definition of the term.

On the surface, the da Rocha Barros and Ferro agree that reverie takes the form of *affective pictograms*. However, it seems like Ferro has contributed to the confusion he decries due to his own shifting views. For example, at times he seems to call for a *strict definition* of reverie as an unbidden image presenting itself to the analyst. Further he criticizes Ogden's expanded definition of reverie, without naming him, when he reports how reverie has become something that can mean everything and its opposite. As he states, "It has been understood too broadly so that whatever comes to mind at any time, everything becomes a reverie, everything becomes a dream like state" (Ferro, 2017, p. 76).[10] He concludes, "It has nothing to do with that, reverie is something very specific" (p. 76).[11] Yet in his 2015 book *Reveries*, where he published hundreds of reveries,[12] he includes many different categories of thoughts and very few visual images or *pictograms*. Here are some examples:[13]

- Thinking about death while living is like thinking about life before being born (p. 44)
- Interminable, the buzzing of the flies.
- Why did they not leave him alone instead of picking on him?
- It was hot and humid all around: the smell ever more oppressive.
- Only the shadow of the vultures told him the truth! (p. 55)
- Which is more stupid, the donkey who cannot or the singing master who would like to make her a soprano, but is only disappointed and frustrated after every bray (p. 194).

While one can appreciate the depth of feeling and sagacity in these ideas, they seem to represent the type of thinking about what a reverie is that he also criticizes. Further, as noted earlier, while later in his writings Ferro seemed to embrace the idea *that the analyst's unspoken reverie was enough for helping the patient to change beta to alpha elements he also embraced a view* (ibid.) *similar to the da Rocha Barros on the need for elaboration of reveries in a language understandable for the patient*: "all the reveries, all the images stored by the assumptive-transformative process of our mind have to be linked, connected, rendered coherent in a *narration* that can be shared with the patient...." (p. XV). Yet still at other times Ferro (2017) minimizes the importance of words, especially when working with the more primitive parts of the personality. For example, he says in this regard, "therapy happens through the rhythm, which is one of the most important aspects, related to the non-verbal, with projective identification, with other things *well before words* (Ferro & Nicoli, 2017, p. 13, italics added.).

In one way, Ogden's view of reverie is closest to Bion's. That is, like Bion's view that the mother's reveries of the infant changes beta into alpha elements, Ogden believes that if he is in a *state of reverie* (as I sense is true in all his clinical examples), *whatever he thinks or does will change beta into alpha elements*. As noted earlier, Ogden's view of reverie is much broader than that of the da Rocha Barros and Ferro (sometimes). His view raises various issues. First of all, Ogden considers reverie a *state of mind* that he believes he goes into where everything is a reverie, while for the da Rocha Barros and *early* Ferro, reverie is something that appears suddenly, and unexpectedly, in the form of an image. Given the power of the unconscious on an analyst's mind I don't believe Ogden's view is sustainable. To accept his view one would have to believe in a perfectly analyzed analyst whose thoughts are totally attuned to the patient's unconscious. Another issue central to Ogden's work is whether it is necessary and useful to distinguish between the analyst's *reveries, countertransference reactions, and associations?* It is ironic that Ogden contributes to what led Bion to create his new language (i.e., the plethora of meanings associated with psychoanalytic concepts). As noted earlier the da Rocha Barros and Ferro make a sharp distinction between countertransference reactions and reverie, and Ferro develops his own term (i.e., narrative derivatives) for what has been called the analyst's free associations. It seems to me that it is important to keep the distinctions noted by da Rocha Barros and Ferro (sometimes), as we are talking about *different states of mind* underlying reverie, free association and counter-transference reactions. The basis of countertransference reactions is unconscious affects, associations most often occur in a *preconscious verbal* form, and reveries occur as *images*, anywhere from *the preconscious to the unconscious*. To call these different mental states, in different parts of the mind, the same thing, would be just the thing Bion decried. There is more to be said about this, but I will reserve it for a later Chapter.

Notes

1 Memories travel along specific neuronal pathways. The more complex these neuronal pathways become the more time an individual has to reflect before acting.

2 The trauma as defined by da Silva was that due to an accident when Joquim was two years-old, he was left alone for several hours. His parents also had difficulty containing their guilt feelings.

3 From this perspective, the middle-age man in the commercial was a wish and denial of my actual age.

4 While some patients find it hard to begin a session and may talk in this fashion, this wasn't an atypical way of talking for this patient throughout his sessions.

5 Early psychoanalytic studies by Escalona (1963) showed, a successful-enough mother with one kind of infant may not be so successful with another type infant.

6 Ogden (2010) noted "The mother, in a state of reverie, accepts the infant's unthinkable thoughts and unbearable feelings (which are inseparable from her response to the infant's distress)" (p. 330).

7 It isn't that the infant understands these words, but it is more the tone of voice. I am reminded of a cartoon I once saw about what dogs hear. The man is saying to the dog, "Well Fido I see it's time for your dinner and then, Fido, we'll take a walk. Sound good to you Fido?" And the dog hears, "blah, blah, blah, Fido, blah, blah, blah, Fido".

8 I have written previously (Busch, 2014) about the usefulness of the underutilized technique of clarification in psychoanalytic treatment.

9 I am using the term reliability here in its scientific sense…i.e., a consistency of results or meanings.

10 This is exactly how Ogden presents reveries.

11 He goes on to highlight the image that comes to mind that is insistent and grating. This raises the interesting question of the affect accompanying reveries, and whether they are important. I will take this up in a later chapter.

12 It isn't clear from the book whose reveries he's reporting, his or his patients' or both.

13 Picked for brevity.

7

QUESTIONS ABOUT REVERIE AS CO-CONSTRUCTED

It has been an important contribution to understanding the analytic situation to realize that, at certain times, we have to be aware of the possibility that what is going on is co-constructed. Most psychoanalysts agree with Pine (2011) that the mind is both "'internally driven and relationally responsive" (p. 825). It is especially helpful to remember a possible co-constructed enactment when stalemates develop, or a patient develops a sudden regression, and other phenomena. However, Ogden and Ferro (in his later years) have proposed the view that *all* analyses, and thus all reveries, are *entirely* co-constructed. With Ferro's (2009) belief in the powers of the "field", the analyst's responsibility for his own thoughts becomes increasingly irrelevant. "In the analytic field, the "subjective fields" of each participant flow together, giving a rise to a new entity that is much more than the sum of its predecessors" (Ferro & Basile, 2009, p. 13) It seems to me that concepts like the field, and analysis as entirely co-constructed, raise various *ethical issues*.

Diamond (2014) recently raised the question of an ethical transgression when the analyst uses his own mental experience in the extreme, forgetting about the patient's psychology and focusing instead on the analyst. Bluntly put, it leaves out the individual psyche of the patient, and the power of the analysand's unconscious to bring about unexpected reactions in the analyst's unconscious that may have *many causes*, some quite idiosyncratic based upon the analyst's own history and subsequent unconscious fantasies, only tangentially related to the patient's unconscious. Therefore, it seems to me, that both from a philosophical and scientific perspective, it seems heuristically necessary to consider a dream as co-constructed as one possibility amongst many.[1]

While Ogden's view of the co-construction of a session is an idea worth considering amongst many, it became for him and many others, the new psychic meaning of the dream in psychoanalysis.

Do we mean the same thing that we did even a decade or two ago when we speak of the patient's dream as 'his' dream? Perhaps it is more accurate to think of the patient's dream as being generated in the context of an analysis (with its own history) consisting of the interplay of the analyst, the analysand and the analytic third, and therefore to consider the dream no longer as simply 'the patient's dream'. In other words, does it any longer make sense to speak of the patient as the dreamer of his dream or are there always several analytic subjects (dreamers) in dialectical tension, each contributing to every analytic construction, even to a psychic event as seemingly personal (i.e. seemingly a production of the workings of the individual unconscious mind) as a dream or a set of dream associations?

(1996, p. 892)

As so much in post-Bionian thinking, this contribution is an important *addition* to how we think about dreams, but leaves out so much of what we know about an individual's capacity to construct his own dreams based upon wishes, defenses, and every psychic mechanism that brings a patient to our office.

Of further interest is that when we hear about some of the post-Bionian's reveries, *we often don't hear about the "co" in the co-creation.* That is, we sometimes (especially Ogden) hear about "reveries" an analyst is having, but not what may have been unconsciously stirred up in the analyst to have these particular thoughts or feelings. This would be the "co" part of a co-created reverie. Instead we have an *a priori* assumption promulgated by some post-Bionians that a reverie *is* co-constructed. Further, we have the view presented by some post-Bionians that the analyst's reactions, no matter how primitive, are part of a co-created reverie that is *containing* for the patient.

It seems to me that the da Rocha Barros' more modest view of the analyst's reveries exemplifies a most fruitful approach. That is, in their view reverie "is a basic tool for *building an interpretation* of the meaning of the emotional experience that happens between the analyst–analysand" (da Rocha Barros and da Rocha Barros, 2016, p. 141). In this way the da Rocha Barros see a reverie as the *beginning of understanding*, not understanding in itself. There is excellent evidence of this in a presentation by Elias da Rocha Barros (2018), and in a contribution by Cassorla (2013). Of course the larger psychoanalytic literature is filled with examples where the analyst uses his associations to help him understand a surprising feeling (e.g., Jacobs, 1993; Aisenstein, 2007).

Many others have pointed to the difficulties in considering all of what is going on in analysis as co-constructed. Eagle (2003) critiqued this position by pointing out "there is the danger that the very existence of the patient's mind structured independently of the analyst is called into question…" (p. 422). I would add the same danger exists for how the analyst thinks of his own mind. As Cassorla (2013) stated, "It is important to note that even though the analyst's dream is part of a *dream-for two,* [2] it is a dream of his or her own" (p. 204). *To put the point more sharply, in some current views of reverie the analyst forgoes responsibility for his own thoughts.* This is especially the case when the analyst believes every thought or feeling he has is a reverie. Katz (2016) taking up Ogden's position says, "All of the experiences of the analyst in the session becomes the material of reverie and of possible relevance to the work" (p. 87). She then adds, "This assumes the analyst is free from pressing worries and other personal disturbances" (p. 87). But how can the analyst know if he is free from personable disturbances? While we may be aware of being a bit depressed or manic, or worried about a child's first day of school, the unconscious meanings of such disturbances cannot be gleaned unless we do considerable psychoanalytic work. Missing is the *self analytic process* that seems necessary to sort through the multiple possibilities of what might be causing us to think a surprising or disturbing thought or feeling. Freud gave us a method, free association, to help us understand not only *what* is on our mind, but *why* that may be. The post-Bionians are brilliant in seeing *what* comes to mind, but by fiat (i.e., believing he or she is in a state of reverie) have pre-empted reflection on *why* what comes to mind comes to mind. *Self-reflection,* [3] *with all of its problems as a source of information about what is on our mind, is the analyst's one bulwark against self-deception.* Diamond (2014) captured this position when he stated,

> The analyst's reflections upon his/her mental processes often function like an internal supervisor that disrupts the dyadic fusional patient–analyst connection dominated by imaginary identification. This unique psychic activity on *mind use* by the analyst in relation to the patient, analyst, and analytic couple—often facilitated by consultants when the capacity for it is lost or blocked—remains a constant, essential factor in the complex process of therapeutic action.
>
> *(p. 533, italics in original)*

In support, Barratt (2017) has recently argued that

> only free-association methodically opens the discourse of self-consciousness (the representations available to reflective awareness) to the voicing of the repressed. The method is key to Freud's originality and the *sine qua non* of any genuinely psychoanalytic process. Clinical procedures which do not prioritize a steadfast and ongoing commitment to this method (instead emphasizing either interpretative formulations, as decisive acts that appear to fix and finalize the meaning of a particular lived experience, or the vicissitudes of transference–countertransference in the immediate treatment situation) all too readily entrap the treatment, limiting its capacity to divulge the power of unconscious processes.
>
> *(p. 39)*

Sara and Cesar Botella (2013), along with Birksted-Breen (2012), describe the necessity of time for reflection to understand an image that suddenly appears. This view is closer to Bion's view of reverie, which can only be understood some time after it has happened. In an example from the Botellas (2013), after a surprising image occurs in a session, followed by a sense of conviction that this image was decisive for the treatment:

I allowed myself some time before intervening. Putting some distance in this way allows the analyst's ego to recover its usual position which, in turn, reduces the state of regrediance, or even causes it to disappear. My usual way of listening, using *free floating association*, returned.

(Botella & Botella, 2013, p. 11, italics added)

If we've learned anything from psychoanalysis it's that anything can mean anything. Therefore, as indicated above, I believe it is only through the analyst's continued exploration of what is on his mind via associations that helps to sort through the meanings of what comes to mind. Below is an example of how my use of associative processes were central to my understanding of a reverie, differentiating it from other possibilities. Many others have reported similar ways of thinking about understanding surprising images that come to mind. This is especially the case in the work of Cassorla (2013) and Birksted-Breen (2012)

Mr. A

In this example I show how my associations to a surprising image become the basis for sorting out what is my contribution to the image, what is the patient's and what is ours. For me it is a necessary process to sort out the significance of what I consider an essential addition from the da Rocha Barros' and early Ferro, the affective pictogram. I see it as an absolute necessity for knowing how to respond to the patient. Thus in response to an unbidden image that is perplexing, it is only via a series of associations that I am able to sort through why I might have had this image, and then how it might be related to Mr. A's treatment and a particular countertransference. It was only via my associations and reflections upon them that I was able to contain what was the beginning of an enactment, and make an unsaturated clarification that led to the patient finding his analytic mind with a series of associations he hadn't had before. The co-constructed nature of the *reverie only becomes clear via the analyst's associations and a growing awareness of a transference–countertransference enactment.*

Clinical material

It was the last session before a two-week vacation break, with termination in the air in a few months. I say it this way, "termination in the air", because although Mr. A had set a date for termination, he would intermittently say this date was too soon or that he knew he could continue to learn a lot if he didn't stop. In my experience this is not an infrequent feeling during termination, and each time it came up we were able to analyze another element of its meaning. Yet the feeling persisted, although both of us felt Mr. A had made significant progress in analysis. From all external signs, Mr. A's life was going very well, and my own psychoanalytic criteria for termination (Busch, 2014) were met. I remained puzzled about the persistence of Mr. A's feeling that it may be too soon to terminate, and realized something more about this needed to be understood.

In this session before the break he began by talking about the upcoming separation, and its meaningfulness in terms of termination, but in an abstract fashion. As we had analyzed, at great length, this intellectualized way of talking about what, at one level seemed meaningful to him, and there seemed to be nothing new emerging, I found myself withdrawing into passive silence. I was listening but not hearing him. While this was a familiar transference–countertransference reaction, it seemed to me that to wonder about it with him now, would have had a routinized, abstract quality. I wasn't sure if this was accurate or a result of *my* withdrawn state.

It was at this point I had an image of one of the great baseball players of all time, Sandy Koufax. Koufax played for a baseball team the "Brooklyn Dodgers", for whom I was a passionate, devoted fan. Koufax was an iconic figure for many Dodger fans as he was born in Brooklyn, and was one of the very few Jewish baseball players at the time. However, the way Koufax came to my mind at that point in the session was with *a feeling of regret*. I wondered why I wasn't more aware and involved with his great achievements when he was one of the best pitchers in baseball history? I then remembered that while Koufax showed potential when he was in Brooklyn, his great achievements occurred only after the team suddenly moved to Los Angeles. Like many, I had never forgiven them for this move to Los Angeles. As one headline in the *New York Times* stated at the time of the move, "They Took Our Hearts Too". I had known from my own analysis that this feeling of betrayal and loss in response to the abrupt move of the Dodgers from Brooklyn to Los Angeles was an important symbol for other personal losses in my adolescence. I had a vague awareness of this connection at the time, but there was some resistance on my part to fully recognize the connection with Mr. A terminating.

My thoughts then turned to a keynote paper I was to give in a week at the meetings of the International Psychoanalytic Association, and some very favorable reviews of my recent book that had just appeared. Was this my Sandy Koufax moment? I wondered at the time if this was reparative…i.e., a narcissistic response to a feeling of loss?

My next thoughts were how Koufax's appeared diminutive in size, but he was actually tall but skinny. It dawned on me that Mr. A was also skinny, and while he had already accomplished a lot before he entered psychoanalysis, he became internationally known in his field during analysis. He had indeed become the Sandy Koufax of his profession. I wondered then if it was *me* who was regretful that I wasn't feeling more about the end of Mr. A's analysis. I finally realized this was the case, and that when Mr. A would occasionally want to put off termination as he felt he wasn't ready, and still had much to learn, I would sometimes muse to myself that I hoped he would change his mind, and stay on. This led me to be able to consider the possibility that Mr. A's concerns about terminating were, in part, an unconscious response to my barely conscious feeling that I didn't want him to terminate.

After these reflections, I found myself more engaged with Mr. A, and tried to find a way to say something about what was going on in the session that might reflect our mutual withdrawal from the feelings involved. What I ended up offering was an unsaturated clarification, "While termination is very much in the air, it seems somewhat removed from both of us." Mr. A then reported that as he was talking he began to feel that his thoughts seemed abstract, and he realized he wasn't feeling connected to his thoughts or me. Mr. A then remembered a time when his father was dying and he regretted not telling him how much he loved him. He then had a memory that had not come up before in the analysis. He thought he was about five or six, and he would feel anxious when going to sleep. He remembered calling his mother who would come in and stroke his back. He briefly became lost in the memory, and then suddenly wondered if he was really anxious at the time, or whether this was a way to get his mother to come in and do this. He laughed in surprise at this thought. He then found himself thinking of needing to get a haircut after our appointment, and what a pain it was to take the time. He then had another memory that he had previously, but this time with a new twist. He had often talked about how his mother had treated him like a self-object (not his words), and took him to the barbershop to get a haircut every two weeks so he would look neat and clean like she wanted him to be. At first, he brought up this memory as a burden, but then he remembered, with gusto, for the first time, that after his hair was cut, the barber would take a hand-held massager, and massage his head. He then reminded me that his current hairdresser is a woman, who often leans up against him with her a body while cutting his hair. She also massages his head when shampooing his hair. "What a burden" he said with a laugh.

I said, "So maybe we can see how your discomfort in feeling connected with me before our separation is that these feelings are tinged with erotic feelings toward this guy who you come to four times a week for a different kind of head massage."

His thoughts turned toward a time when his mother was quite sick and no one could figure out what was wrong with her. In a new memory, he recalled that after one doctor came she started to feel better. At the time, he imagined the doctor had bitten into her and sucked the illness out of her. He wondered if he ever connected that with her later mental illness. He then reflected on the fact that he just did. I then said, "Even more reason to keep yourself distant from this massage doctor who supposedly is trying to help you."

Reflections

As Green (1992) stated, "The capacity for reverie is merely the visible aspect of a largely unconscious form of thought" (p. 586). If this is the case, how do we understand the unconscious meaning of a reverie? In this session, I have a spontaneous image that appeared unbidden, an affective pictogram. Was this a co-constructed image, involving our two preconscious or unconscious minds? Was it produced to help transform the patient's beta into alpha elements? Or was some other intrapsychic or interpsychic process involved? How can we answer such questions? As indicated above, I believe we should rely on our self-analytic methods, noticing our associations and reflecting and playing with them. I don't believe that one can decide by fiat that any image or thought is a reverie.

In my understanding, the reverie (affective pictogram) I have in the session, *along with my associations to the reverie*, lead me to better analyze and integrate my *feelings* about Mr. A's impending termination. That is, my *thoughts* about hoping he might stay in analysis were conscious, but the intensity of my *feelings* about it had been split off. I couldn't say why they were split off at the time, but in retrospect I realized that it was also a time when I was contemplating limiting my practice by not taking on any new analytic patients, and thus I was dealing with another type of loss. Of course, there was also a personal characteristic of mine, a stoic response to loss and injury that contributed to my splitting off from my feelings at the time. Putting all this together led me to realize that Mr. A's expressed thoughts about his reluctance to terminate were likely, in part, a response to my ambivalent feelings about his termination.

When I re-gained my analytic mind, Mr. A's associations reminded us, that in psychoanalysis, there is rarely only one meaning to anything. Thus, in a surprising turn, Mr. A feels regret about his not fully mourning the death of his father. While his regret may have contributed to the regret I felt that accompanied the Koufax image, it is also tinged with oedipal guilt as Mr. A remembers calling his mother to his bedroom. However, his laughing about the recognition that he may not have been feeling that anxious suggests a freedom to tolerate previously warded off thoughts and feelings, which leads to additional memories, told with gusto, of erotic and homoerotic excitement, leading to the recalling for the first time, of his mother's cure of one illness by the sucking doctor, leading to mental illness.

What I want to emphasize in these associations is that Mr. A has found his psychoanalytic mind, which I consider one of the primary factors in thinking that psychoanalysis has done what it is meant to do (Busch, 2014). That is, the patient has gained the freedom to free associate, and to reflect upon these associations to begin to understand their meaning.

As a reminder, I bring this vignette as a way of showing how complex it seems to understand the meaning of a reverie. Why should it be different? Using the affective pictogram as a concept that best captures a reverie, it is useful to remember it is the *beginning articulation in the analyst's mind of a symbolic understanding*, and like with any beginning, further work is needed for its full articulation. It is my impression that this further understanding can mainly be gleaned through the analyst's own associations. From this perspective, it is hard to endorse the idea that the analyst's reveries, by themselves, are primarily transformative for the patient.

In short, I bring this example, familiar to many psychoanalysts in the 21st century, as a way of sorting through the unbidden images (feelings and thoughts) that come to the analyst's mind during an analytic session. *It is a way of working that is different than some post-Bionians who, by definition, view every reverie as co-constructed.* In my understanding, it is only through my own associations in conjunction with what I become aware of in the transference–countertransference that allowed me to see the co-constructed nature of the image of Sandy Koufax, and the feeling of regret that accompanied it. Both Mr. A and myself were having difficulty recognizing the good work we had done, and the resistance to separation.

Bion seemed to believe that associations were the main way to understand a psychic event.

> This patient had begun occasionally to report dreams to me. It was a comparatively recent development, some three or four months only, *but in the absence of associations I had not felt able to make much headway* beyond a few somewhat obvious suggestions such as that he felt it was something important to tell me or that he felt I would be the kind of person who understood them.
>
> *(Bion, 1958, p. 345, italics added)*

I believe a more honest position on the meanings of images or feelings that come unbidden is expressed by Jacobs (1983), when he states:

> Unpleasant or painful affects may stimulate in the analyst defensive operations aimed at eliminating them or reducing their intensity. Thus, the evocation in the analyst of self- and object-linked memories creates in him a dynamic state in which certain reawakened affects, wishes, and superego responses give rise to the employment of those defensive operations originally used against them. When an imbalance in this dynamic process occurs, either from the side of defense or from the side of the resurgent forces, the stage is set for the appearance of overt countertransference reactions.
>
> *(p. 633)*

This is exemplified in an earlier study by Kern (1978), where visual images stimulated during analytic sessions, were found to be *indications of unconscious attempts to obscure, misunderstand, and deflect the patient and myself from the analytic work.* They were indications of unconscious countertransference, the forms of which contained both transferred fragments of conflictual early object relations *and* projected early self-representations.

As early as 1962 Ross and Kapp reported that the *visual images* that "pop" into the analyst's mind appear to be an instance of the unconscious activity of the analyst's mind, caught as a snapshot, in the process of responding to the unconscious activity of the patient's mind. However, their way of dealing with these visual images was to allow themselves to associate to them, leading to the conclusion that these images often helped them understand *unconscious countertransferences.* Here is one example they present:

> A woman patient who had made considerable progress earlier in her analysis had been in the analytic doldrums for several weeks before the dream to be noted. Despite the fact that the analyst had interpreted the conflicts around her erotic transference many times, she could not recognize these feelings. The lack of movement in the analysis and the ineffectiveness of his interpretations were clues to the analyst that there probably was some sort of countertransference resistance.

At this time in the analysis the patient dreamed she was sitting in her dinette with a person whose identity was vague. A woman friend of the patient, who was also in analysis, and who seemed to be living in the same house, came into the room looking ill and said that she was planning to move away. So, the dream ended.

While the patient was telling the dream the analyst suddenly visualized a certain dinette from his own recent social experiences. Free association by the analyst to the dinette he had visualized led to a woman the analyst often met socially and whom, frankly, he would have liked to meet much less often because he considered her social behavior to be that of a superficial flirt, a bore, and someone who constantly was demanding various favors from him. He next recalled a woman who had been the housekeeper in the home where he lived as a child. She had been devoted to him but he had gradually come to dislike her because of her stubbornness and her excessive demands on him to reciprocate her love. When she became unhappy in her job and quit, he had been pleased.

Through such associations, the analyst began to consider the possibility that subtly and unconsciously he had been encouraging the patient to defend herself against the erotic transference by leaving treatment. It now became clear to him why his previous attempts to interpret the transference had been clumsy and unsuccessful. His unconscious countertransference feeling was one of wanting the patient to leave treatment. Before the analyst recognized these feelings, his interpretations, colored by unconscious feelings of wanting to reject the patient, had been presented in a manner which contributed to the patient feeling that she was being criticized and excluded by her therapist. Once this was clear, the analyst was able to deal with the transference neurosis in a constructive manner and the analysis progressed again. The patient could now accept the nonrejecting clarification of her erotic feelings to the analyst. These feelings and the defenses against them no longer constituted a resistance to analytic movement.

(pgs. 647–648)

Here, once again, one can see how the analyst's associations to an image help him understand a countertransference. It seems to me that this is the very least we must do to fully understand our reveries. Diamond (2014) captured what I consider the *standard* by which the analyst's mental activity in understanding his patient needs to be evaluated. According to Diamond "the analyst must":

1. Allow for *regression in ego functioning*;
2. *Take his/her own mind as an object,* including its manifestation in the analyst third;
3. *Contain internal experience,* including bearing uncertainty and tolerating intense affective states;
4. *Utilize more developed ego functions* for self-reflexivity and elaboration. (p. 548, italics in original).

In closing, I think Bolognini (2004) encapsulated the essence of the psycho-analyst's task, but *overestimated its acceptance,* when he stated:

There are, in fact, no real differences of opinion on the next step either, that is on the general principle that the patient's intrapsychic changes are *also* the result of work *on* the patient's interpsychic *with* that same patient's intrapsychic (development of transference, stream of associations, re-emergence of memories, insight and so on) and *with* the analyst's intrapsychic (analysis of his own transference and countertransference, the use of his associations, memories and so on to formulate interpretations).

(p. 337)

Notes

1 Further, it is a return to a type of thinking before the development of Cartesian doubt (primarily known through the work of Descartes). In Cartesian doubt, skepticism about one's beliefs is a way of determinining the likelihood of their greater accuracy. Sensory experience, in particular, is viewed as often erroneous. What is described as the dream argument postulates that the dream is used as preliminary evidence that the senses we trust in distinguishing reality from fantasy *should at least be carefully examined* to determine whether is in fact reality.

2 As described by Cassorla (2013), "The analyst's dream, implied or told to the patient through interpretation, may then be absorbed, in turn, by the patient may connect to the patient's symbolic network, and may be re-dreamed by the patient. This new dream of the patient is told to the analyst who then may re-dream it, and so on" (p. 204).

3 By self-reflection I mean musing and dreaming one's thoughts, not thinking real hard about something.

8

CONCEPTUALIZING AN ENIGMA

The title of this Chapter captures the difficulty of what I will be attempting. However, I push on thinking there is a way of conceptualizing the analyst's reveries that might bring some order to how we might think about them. The difficulty of the task will be captured in the multiple caveats I present along the way. I am not presenting what I consider a definite classification of reverie, but a guideline to help us think about it. Let me first reiterate what has led me to believe there is an important need to classify the analyst's reveries.

While the analyst's reveries will remain an important addition to the psychoanalyst's way of understanding, in many current formulations it remains confused and limiting, requiring more exploration. Some of its proponents have presented it as a new royal road into the patient's unconscious, suggesting significant paradigm changes in the curative process, while folding into its definition concepts that have long had their own meanings (e.g., countertransference). It has led, for some to a rejection of the self-analytic work an analyst needs to do to understand his reactions to a patient, especially when his feelings are intense. Instead what we see for some post-Bionians is a reliance on what I have called (Busch, 2014), the *Descartian Somersault*, where self-analysis is replaced by a radical *subjectivity*, not a co-constructed one, characterized by a position of *I think therefore you are*. Further, some of the more extreme post-Bionian proposals seem based on limited data. It is often difficult to tell what transformation has taken place, and how the analyst's "reverie" (especially somatic reactions) has led to these murky transformations.

My views are based on Bion's initial idea of a reverie's transforming properties, and the post-Bionians' view of reverie as a dream-like state. In general, I start from the perspective that transforming the under-represented into something potentially representable or represented in a more complex form is a cornerstone of the psychoanalytic curative process. Using levels of *psychic representation* as a guide, I think one can build *a hierarchy of the analyst's reveries based upon their transformative potential*.

That is, the more psychically complex the analyst's reverie, the greater is the chance it can help the analyst elaborate a representation for the patient. For example, the analyst's bodily sensations (clenched stomach), feeling states. perceptions (sounds, smells), and sensations have the potential to lead the analyst to an understanding of something not yet known, but they are in a more *primitive form of representation than, for example, the affective pictogram,* and thus still need significant analytic work before they become transformed into something representable for the analyst, and thus potentially transformative for the patient.

We would then have the following classifications.

1. *The affective pictogram, as described by Elias and Elizabeth da Rocha Barros, seems the ideal way to conceptualize a reverie.* This is because:

    a   It fits best with Bion's original definition of reverie as a *beginning* transformation of *beta* to *alpha* elements.

    b   An affective pictogram already comes to the analyst as a *representation* of something that neither the analyst nor analysand was aware of. *As it is already a representation,* a *process of transformation has already begun in the analyst's mind.*

    c   *It is a new form of representation (i.e., visual image) different then from countertransference reactions, where the analyst may feel something (i.e., depressed, feverish, excited, etc.), or free associations that come in the form of verbally transcribed memories (i.e., a joke, thoughts about a dying friend, an interpretation by our own analyst).* Further it represents something (i.e., unconscious conflict, fantasy, repair of a self-state, projection) not previously known by the analyst that comes unbidden in this unique form. The image is a representation that is closest to the dream state that the post-Bionians are trying to capture. The image is a creative act, much like an artistic production described by Kris as early as 1938 as a "regression in the service of the ego" (p. 290).

    d   Thinking in pictures starts to develop around age two (Flavell et al., 2002), when there has been a certain growth of the ego. This "picture thinking", as a beginning representation, would seem to stand somewhere between Freud's (1915) idea of "thing presentations" and "word presentations".

2. By definition, the *affective pictogram* has a feeling associated with it. It would make sense that the quality of the feeling associated with the affective pictogram would have something to do with its transformational potential. That is, an image filled with dread that the analyst has a hard time holding onto would be more difficult to translate into a representation than one associated with neutral or positive feelings.

3. I would rule out *somatic states* as reveries, as they seem to be the *antithesis of psychic elaboration.* I agree with Aisenstein (2017) who characterizes somatic patients as those who defend against thinking or picturing things. French psychoanalysts have observed that psychosomatic states are associated with "severe deficiencies in fantasy life and a thinking bound to the concrete" (Lecours and Bouchard, 1997, p. 857). As a reminder, Ferro considers somatic states as an evacuation of beta elements.

Feeling states: While feeling states, like sadness or excitement, are usually characterized by the immediacy of the experience, if there is some degree of psychic elaboration it can be recognized as something different than blank spaces or undifferentiated states.

Perceptions: This includes things like olfactory or auditory perceptions. They can be the beginning elaboration of a psychic state, although in more primitive forms they can become a psychotic hallucination. *However, we also might consider that certain analysts have a proclivity for perceptual alignments with the patient's unconscious that allows them a greater capacity for elaboration than most of us.*

Images: In the realm of the analyst's reveries this is at the highest level of psychic elaboration in that it is already a symbolic representation.

Words, in the form of free associations, *can be* the result of deep and symbolized representations. However, I wouldn't put them in the category of reveries, which are supposed to hold a transformative *potential*, while free associations are already the result of a process of transformation that has taken place. As far as I can tell Ferro (e.g., 2002b) uses the term *narrative* as an equivalent to associations. "The way in which the patient 'hears' this interpretation is "pictographed" in an alpha element and a sequence of alpha elements. These elements cannot be known directly. They are, however, somehow made knowable by "narrative derivatives", that is, by the patient's "discourse" immediately following the interpretation (p. 185).

I consider unbidden *affective pictogram* as coming closest to what Bion attempted to elucidate, while also having the most transformative potential. I am also in favor of the da Rochas Barros' *affective pictogram* rather than Ferro's *pictogram* in that the affect that accompanies an image may reflect where along the pre-conscious–unconscious dimension the image is coming from, and thus roughly specify the amount of self-analytic work the analyst will have to do to effectively use the image. *An affective pictogram that causes the analyst discomfort and is difficult to hold onto is more likely a representation filled with more highly defended unconscious meaning than a neutral or pleasurable one.* This may help us understand something pointed out earlier...i.e., the post-Bionians' seeming confusion in sometimes describing the analyst's reverie as based in the *pre-conscious,* and at other times as something based in the analyst's *unconscious.* While there has been no commentary from the post-Bionians indicating they were describing reveries as occurring in different parts of the mind, they were picking up on something important, that the analyst's reveries are formed in different parts of the mind, and are associated with different affects upon being received by the analyst.

In general, then, different mental states as potential reveries can be placed along a *continuum of degrees of representation*, from the primitive to more symbolic. Further, the more primitive the feeling state or thought the more difficult it will be for the analyst to sort out: (1) what is co-created; (2) what is something understood about the patient's mental life; and (3) what is the analyst's idiosyncratic reaction. Further there seems little doubt that the more primitive the analyst's reaction, the harder it will be to know how to translate it into something useful for the patient. Ogden's description of his somatic states is an example of a more primitive feeling that is difficult to translate.

Bodily feelings as a very primitive form of representation are there from the beginning of life. However, an image suddenly appearing in the analyst's mind is an advancement from a feeling state or perception in that it is already a representation. However, there are various questions I think would be useful to consider in thinking about the *affective pictograms* viewed by the da Rochas Barros as the quintessential reverie. To sum up my questions:

1. What is the quality of the affect associated with the pictogram? Images that come to mind during an analytic session fit along a continuum from terrifying to funny, and everything in between.
2. A parallel question regards the stability of the pictogram, and how difficult it is for the analyst to hold on to.
3. In the model I am proposing, the ease with which associations come to mind might also help determine the unconscious depth of a potential reverie. I consider the possibility of *ease of associations to the pictogram as an important criterion in determining whether we translate an image into an interpretation in the session in which it occurs or not*. However, one needs to keep in mind that ease of associations might also represent a manic defense against the affect associated with the image.

These questions touch on the issue of where in the unconscious an image might come from,[1] and thus the difficulty the analyst might have in associating to it, reflecting on it, and making an interpretation that will be of use for the patient. But why does a pictogram appear in the analyst's mind as a form of representation? The image as unconscious begins with Freud (1915) who noted that the unconscious thing presentations are *images*. Thing presentations he said, "consist in the cathexis, if not of the direct *memory-images* of the thing, at least of a remoter memory-trace derived from these" (p. 210, italics added).[2] According to Botella & Botella (2005) "Aulagnier (1975) described the notions of *pictograms* and *pictorial language*" (p. 47) as identical to the *thing image*, thus making an extension and link to Freud's conception. The Botellas note that Freud (1933) drew a parallel in the *New Introductory Lectures* between the absence of affect in dream thoughts and the sensory strength of dream pictures, thus suggesting a defensive process in the formation of pictograms. In short Freudian views of the pictogram match the post-Bionian view of its connection with the unconscious. *However, where in the unconscious an image comes from and its transferability to a representation in words remains to be discovered in each pictogram.*

Further thoughts

It is my impression there has been an unacknowledged shift from Bion's idea of reverie as a kind of *background phenomenon* in the analyst's approach to the patient to the idea of reverie into something *concrete, a state of mind* that can be used by the analyst as the primary method of understanding and treating the patient. It is like this with many who follow the introduction of a new concept, as it is revised and further articulated. Therefore, the post-Bionian views of reverie should be evaluated on their own merits.

For a new term to have validity, it should capture something unique. Bion's original concept of reverie was unique, in that this state of mind of the analyst, and its effect on the patient, had not been articulated previously (Freud's free floating attention comes closest, but it was not seen as having the transforming function (beta into alpha elements) described by Bion.) Many of the ways reverie is presented by some post-Bionians seem to have been described previously by Freud as daydreams, night dreams, and associations. While some post-Bionians view having these thoughts as transformational in themselves, there are many questions that need to be answered about this formulation. As noted earlier, much of what Ogden describes as part of his reveries has been previously observed and categorized differently in the psychoanalytic literature…i.e., somatic reactions, defenses, countertransference, associations etc.

Further, as I have elaborated earlier, the analyst must still reflect on this image to try, as best he can, to distinguish what the image represents…i.e., something new that is understood about the patient, or something stirred in the analyst's unconscious that is more idiosyncratic. With the proper precautions noted earlier, these images have the potential for the analyst to understand something previously not fully known that unlocks new ways of understanding, and thus has the possibility of being transformational for the patient. If we can appreciate an unconscious with depth, that runs from the border of the preconscious to an unfathomable, endless depth (Busch, 2009, 2014), it would seem this image could be a creation from the unconscious that is close enough to the preconscious to form this dream-like image that is capable of becoming conscious. In their contribution, the da Rochas Barros have found a unique way of elaborating reverie that seems to meet the standard of a valid definition. Further their appreciation for the need to translate these affective pictograms into symbolic meaning for the patient leads their work to fit within the framework of the Freudian–Kleinian tradition.

In linking reverie to a state or reaction on the analyst's part in a single session, the post-Bionians have used as their criteria the short-term growth one might see in a session (e.g., a dream). However, it is often difficult to tell if this is the work of the analyst's reverie in the session, or *all the analytic work that has come beforehand.* While this short-term growth may be the building block of structural growth, it can often be limited as the patient regresses and returns to his character-defenses as part of the working though process.

While reading through the post-Bionian literature I kept on being reminded of Weinshel's (1984) appeal for "the elevation of the not-so-good hour", where he makes a plea for the

> increased recognition of and attention to the less glamorous and exciting exchanges that take place daily at the interface of the analyst–analysand interaction, the more prosaic and 'quiet' elements of that interaction, and how the analyst and his interventions assist the patient's analytic efforts—instead of so much attention to those frames in the analytic work which feature the analyst in a starring role.
>
> (pp. 89–90)

It seems to me that what Bion was trying to capture was a background to a good-enough analysis. That is, the many hundreds of ways the analyst's stance serves as a medium for the containment of primitive emotions captured by many analysts as for example in Winnicott's (1965) holding environment, Kohut's (1971) mirroring and self-object function for the narcissistic patient, or the father's role of the analytic third suggested by Green (1975), and many, many others (and the way we talk to a patient, greet them, listen, or consistently seem harried, or start sessions late, or if we bypass strong feelings and drive derivatives).

Notes

1 I'm thinking here of Freud's 1933 drawing of the Structural Model (p. 78) where the unconscious goes from the border with the preconscious to an endless unknown. (See Busch, 2006a, for a discussion of this drawing.)
2 For a more complete discussion see Schmidt-Hellerau (2001, pgs. 139–141).

REFERENCES

Aguayo, J., & Malin, B. (2013). *Los Angeles Seminars and Supervision*. London: Karnac.

Aguayo, J., Pistner de Cortinas, L., & Regeczkey, A. (2018). *Bion in Buenos Aires*. London: Karnac.

Aisenstein, M. (2007). On Therapeutic Action. *Psychoanal. Q*, 76S:1443–1461.

Aisenstein, M. (2017). *An Analytic Journey*. London: Routledge.

Aisenstein, M., & Smadja, C. (2010). Conceptual Framework from the Paris Psychosomatic School: A Clinical Psychoanalytic Approach to Oncology. *Int. J. Psychoanal.*, 91(3):621–640.

Aulagnier, P. (1975). *The Violence of Interpretation*. New York: Bruner-Routledge.

Aulagnier, P. (1984). Le retrait dans l'hallucination: un équivalent du retrait autistique? In *Lieux de l'enfance, 3*. Toulouse: Privat.

Baranger, M., Baranger, W., & Mom, J. M. (1988). The Infantile Psychic Trauma from Us to Freud: Pure Trauma, Retroactivity and Reconstruction. *Int. J. Psychoanal.*, 69:113–128.

Baranger, M., Baranger, W., & Mom, J. (1983). Process and Non-Process in Analytic Work. *Int. J. Psychoanal.*, 64:1–15.

Barratt, B.B. (2017). Opening to the Otherwise. *Int. J. Psychoanal.*, 98:39–53.

Beres, D. (1957). Communication in Psychoanalysis and in the Creative Process: A Parallel. *J. Amer. Psychoanal. Assn.*, 5:408–423.

Bergman, P., & Escalona, S.K. (1949). Unusual Sensitivities in Very Young Children. *Psychoanal. St. Child*, 4:333–352

Bezoari, M., & Ferro, A. (1989). Listening, Interpretations and Transformative Functions in the Analytical Dialogue. *Rivista Psicoanal.*, 35(4):1014–1050.

Bion, W. R. (1962). *Learning from Experience*. London: Tavistock.

Bion, W. R. (1963). *Elements of Psycho-Analysis*. London: Heinemann.

Bion, W. R. (1970). *Attention and Interpretation*. London: Tavistock.

Bion, W.R. (1976). Evidence. In *Clinical Seminars and Other Works*. London: Karnac, pgs. 312–320.

Bion, W.R. (1958). On Hallucination. *Int. J. Psycho-Anal.*, 39:341–349.

Bion, W.R. (1987). *Clinical Seminars and Other Works*. London: Karnac.

Bion, W.R. (1990). *Brazilian Lectures*. London: Karnac.

Bion, W.R. (1991). *Cogitations*. London: Karnac.

Bion, W.R. (2005). *The Italian Lectures*. London: Karnac.

Birksted-Breen, D. (2012). Taking Time: The Tempo of Psychoanalysis. *Int. J. Psycho-Anal.*, 93:819–835.

Birksted-Breen, D. (2016). Bi-occularity the Functioning Mind of the Analyst. *Int. J. Psycho-Anal.*, 97: 25–40.

Bolognini, S. (2004). Intrapsychic-Interpsychic. *Int. J. Psycho-Anal.*, 85:337–358.

Botella, C. & Botella, S. (2005). *The Work of Psychic Figurability*. London: Routledge.

Botella, C., & Botella, S. (2013). Psychic Figurability and Unrepresented States. In Levine, H., Reed, GS, & Scarfone, D. *Unrepresented States and the Construction of Meaning*. London: Karnac.

Bott-Spillius, E. (1994). On Formulating Clinical Facts to a Patient. *Int. J. Psycho-Anal.*, 75: 1121–1132.

Bowlby, J., Robertson, J., & Rosenbluth, D. (1952). A Two-Year-Old Goes to Hospital. *Psychoanal Study Child*, 7:82–94.

Boyer, L. B. (1997). The Verbal Squiggle Game in Treating the Seriously Disturbed Patient. *Psychoanal. Q.*, 66:62–81.

Breuer, J. (1893). Fräulein Anna O, Case Histories from Studies on Hysteria. *S.E.* II:19–47

Breuer, J., & Freud, S. (1893). Studies on Hysteria. *S.E.* II: 1–240.

Brown, L. J. (2009). Bion's Ego Psychology: Implications for an Intersubjective View of Psychic Structure. *Psychoanal. Q.*, 78(1):27–55.

Brown, L. J. (2010). Klein, Bion, and Intersubjectivity: Becoming, Transforming, and Dreaming. *Psychoanal. Dial.*, 20(6):669–682.

Bucci, W. (2001). Pathways of Emotional Communication. *Psychoanal. Inq.*, 21(1):40–70.

Busch, F. (1968). Transference in Psychological Testing. *J. Proj. Techniques*, 32:509–512.

Busch, F. (1993). "In the Neighborhood": Aspects of a Good Interpretation and a "Developmental Lag" in Ego Psychology. *J. Amer. Psychoanal. Assn.*, 41:151–177.

Busch, F. (1995). *The Ego at the Center of Technique*. New York, NY: Rowan and Littlefield.

Busch, F. (1999). *Rethinking Clinical Technique*. New York, NY: Rowan and Littlefield.

Busch, F. (2000). What is a Deep Interpretation?. *J. Amer. Psychoanal. Assn.*, 48(1):237–254.

Busch, F. (2006a). A Shadow Concept. *Int. J. Psycho-Anal.*, 87(6):1471–1485.

Busch, F. (2006b). Countertransference in Defense Enactments. *J. Amer. Psychoanal. Assn.*, 54(1):67–85

Busch, F. (2009). "Can You Push a Camel through the Eye of a Needle?" Reflections on how the Unconscious Speaks to us and its Clinical Implications. *Int. J. Psychoanal.*, 90 (1):53–68.

Busch, F. (2014). *Creating a Psychoanalytic Mind*. London: Routledge.

Busch, F. (2015). Our Vital Profession. *Int. J. Psychoanal.*, 96:553–568.

Busch, F., & Schmidt-Hellerau, C. (2004). How Can we Know what we Need to Know? Reflections on Clinical Judgment Formation. *J. Amer. Psychoanal. Assn.*, 51:689–708.

Cassorla, R. (2013). In Search of Symbolization. In Levine, H., Reed, G. S., & Scarfone, D. *Unrepresented States and the Construction of Meaning*. London: Karnac.

Civitarese, G., & Ferro, A. (2013). The Meaning and Use of Metaphor in Analytic Field Theory. *Psychoanal. Inq.*, 33(3):190–209.

Coltart, N. E. C. (1986). "Slouching towards Bethlehem…" or Thinking the Unthinkable in Psychoanalysis. In *The British School of Psychoanalysis. The Independent Tradition*, ed. G. Kohon, New Haven: Yale University Press, pgs. 185–199.

da Rocha Barros, E. M. (2000). Affect and Pictographic Image. *Int. J. Psycho-Anal.*, 81:1087–1099.

da Rocha Barros, E. M. (2002). An Essay on Dreaming, Psychical Working out and Working Through. *Int. J. Psycho-Anal.*, 83:1083–1093.

da Rocha Barros, E. M., & da Rocha Barros, E. L. (2011). Reflections on the Clinical Implications of Symbolism. *Int. J. Psycho-Anal.*, 92:879–901.

da Rocha Barros, E. M., & da Rocha Barros, E. L. (2016). The Function of Evocation in the Working through of Countertransference: Projective Identification, Reverie, and the Expressive Function of the Mind—Reflections Inspired by Bion's Work. In Levine, H. B. & Civitarese, G. (Eds.), *The W.R. Bion Tradition*. London: Karnac.

da Rocha Barros, E. M., (2018). Symbol Formation and Transformations in Theory and Practice. Presented to the 43rd Annual Conference of the Canadian Psychoanalytic Society. Montreal, June 2018.

da Silva, M. C. (2017). The Analyst's Narrative Function. *Int. J. Psychoanal.*, 98:21–38.

de Mattos, J. A. J. (2016). Impressions of my Analysis with Dr. Bion. In Levine, H. and Civitarese, G. (Eds). *The W.R. Bion Tradition*. London: Karnac.

Diamond, M. J. (2014). Analytic Mind Use and Interpsychic Communication: Driving Force in Analytic Technique, Pathway to Unconscious Mental Life. *Psychoanal. Q.*, 83(3):525–563.

Dickes, R. (1965). The Defensive Function of an Altered State of Consciousness. *J. Amer. Psychoanal. Assn.*, 13:356–403

Eagle, M. N. (2003). The Postmodern Turn in Psychoanalysis: A Critique. *Psychoanal. Psychol.*, 20(3):411–424.

Escalona, S. (1963). *The Roots of Individuality*. Chicago: Aldine Press.

Fédida, P. (1992). *Nome, Figura e Memöria*. São Paulo: Escuta.

Ferro, A. (1992). Two Authors in Search of Characters: The Relationship, the Field, the Story. *Rivista Psicoanal.*, 38:44–90.

Ferro, A. (1993). From Hallucination to Dream: From Evacuation to the Tolerability of Pain in the Analysis of a Preadolescent. *Psychoanal. Rev.*, 80(3):389–404.

Ferro, A. (2002a). Some Implications of Bion's Thought. *Int. J. Psycho-Anal.*, 83:597–607.

Ferro, A. (2002b). Narrative Derivatives of Alpha Elements. *Int. Forum Psychoanal.*, 11:184–187.

Ferro, A. (2002c). *In the Analyst's Consulting Room*. London: Bruner-Routledge.

Ferro, A. (2005). Four Sessions with Lisa. *Int. J. Psycho-Anal.*, 86:1247–1256.

Ferro, A. (2006). Clinical Implications of Bion's Thought. *Int. J. Psycho-Anal.*, 87:989–1003.

Ferro, A. (2008). The Patient as the Analyst's Best Colleague: Transformation into a Dream and Narrative Transformations. *The Italian Psychoanalytic Annual*, 2:199–205.

Ferro, A. (2009). *Mind Works*. London: Routledge.

Ferro, A. (2015). *Reveries*. London: Karnac.

Ferro, A. (2016). Changes in Technique and in the Theory of Technique in a Post-Bionian Field Model. In Levine, H. B. & Civitarese, G. (Eds.), *The W.R. Bion Tradition*. London: Karnac.

Ferro, A., & Basile, R. (2008). Countertransference and the Characters of the Psychoanalytic Session. *Scand. Psychoanal. Rev.*, 31(1):3–10.

Ferro, A., & Basile, R. (2009). The Universe of the Field and its Inhabitants. In Ferro & Basile (Eds.), *The Analytic Field*. London: Karnac.

Ferro, A., & Nicoli, L. (2017) *The New Analyst's Guide to the Galaxy*. London: Karnac Books.

Flannery, J. G. (1979). Dimensions of a Single Word-Association in the Analyst's Reverie. *Int. J. Psychoanal.*, 60:217–223.

Flavell, J. H., Miller, P. H., & Miller, S. A. (2002) *Cognitive Development*. Upper-Saddle, NJ: Prentice-Hall.

Frayn, D. H. (1987). An Analyst's Regressive Reverie: A Response to the Analysand's Illness. *Int. J. Psychoanal.*, 68:271–277.

Freud, S. (1910). Wild Psycho-Analysis. *S.E.* XI:219–228.

Freud, S. (1911). Formulations on the Two Principles of Mental Functioning. *S.E.* XII:213–226.

Freud, S. (1912). Recommendations to Physicians Practising Psycho-Analysis. *S.E.* XII:109–120.

Freud, S. (1914). Remembering, Repeating and Working-Through (Further Recommendations on the Technique of Psycho-Analysis II). *S.E.* XII:145–156.

Freud, S. (1915). The Unconscious. *S.E.* XIV:166–216.

Freud, S. (1916). Some Character-Types Met with in Psycho-Analytic Work. *S.E.* XIV: 309–333.

Freud, S. (1923). The Ego and the Id. *S.E.* XIX:1–66.

Freud, S. (1926). Inhibitions, Symptoms and Anxiety. *S.E.* XX:75–176.

Freud, S. (1933). New Introductory Lectures on Psychoanalysis. *S.E.* XXII:1–182.

Gray, P. (1994). *The Ego and Analysis of Defense*. New York: Aronson.

Green, A. (1974). Surface Analysis, Deep Analysis. *Int. Rev. Psychoanal.*, 1:415–423.

Green, A. (1975). The Analyst, Symbolization and Absence in the Analytic Setting (On Changes in Analytic Practice and Analytic Experience). In Memory of D. W. Winnicott. *Int. J. Psychoanal.*, 56:1–22.

Green, A. (1992). Cogitations. *Int. J. Psycho-Anal.*, 73:585–589.

Grinberg, L. (1987). Dreams and Acting Out. *Psychoanal. Q.*, 56:155–176.

Grotstein, J. (2000). *Who Is the Dreamer Who Dreams the Dream?* Hillsdale, NJ: Analytic Press.

Grotstein, J. (2007). *A Beam of Intense Darkness. Wilfred Bion's Legacy to Psychoanalysis*. London: Karnac.

Grotstein, J. (2009). *But at the Same Time and at Another Level*. London: Karnac.

Hartmann, H. (1939). *Ego Psychology and the Problem of Adaptation*. New York: International Universities Press, Inc.

Hermon, N. (2016). On Becoming a Child: Reverie in the Psychotherapy of Children. *Int. J. Psycho-Anal.*, 97(6):1591–1608.

Horner, T., Whiteside, M., & Busch, F. (1976b). The Mutual Influence of the Positive Cohesive Self, Mental Representational Structures, and Interactive Behavior in the Child's Involvement with Peers. *Int. J. Psychoanal.*, 57:461–475.

Jacobs, T. J. (1983). The Analyst and the Patient's Object World: Notes on an Aspect of Countertransference. *J. Amer. Psychoanal. Assn.*, 31:619–642.

Jacobs, T. J. (1993). The Inner Experiences of the Analyst: Their Contribution to the Analytic Process. *Int. J. Psycho-Anal.*, 74:7–14.

Jacobson, E. (1954). The Self and the Object World. *Psychoanal. St. Child*, 9:75–127.

Katz, S. M. (2016). The Timing of the Use of Reverie. In Buie, D. & Harrong, C., *From Reverie to Interpretation*. London: Karnac.

Kern, J. W. (1978). Countertransference and Spontaneous Screens: An Analyst Studies his Own Visual Images. *J. Amer. Psychoanal. Assn.*, 26:21–47.

Kernberg, O. (2017). Review of *Wilford Bion: Los Angeles Seminars* (Aguayo, J. & Malin, B. Eds.). *Int. J. Psycho-Anal.*, 98: 250–225.

Kohut, H. (1971). *The Analysis of the Self*. New York: Int. Univ. Press.

Kris, E. (1936). The Psychology of Caricature. *Int. J. Psycho-Anal.*, 17:285–303.

Lecours, S., & Bouchard, M-A. (1997). Dimensions of Mentalization. *Int. J. Psychoanal.*, 78:855–875.

Lecours, S. (2007). Supportive Interventions and Nonsymbolic Mental Functioning. *Int. J. Psychoanal.*, 88(4):895–915.

Levine, H., & Civitarese, G. (Eds.) (2016). *The W.R. Bion Tradition*. London: Karnac.

Levine, H. B., & Reed, G. (2015). Prologue: Responses to the Work of Antonino Ferro. *Psychoanal. Inq.*, 35(5):449–450.

Loewald, H. W. (1971). Some Considerations on Repetition and Repetition Compulsion. *Int. J. Psychoanal.*, 52:59–66.

Loewald, H. W. (1975). Psychoanalysis as an Art and the Fantasy Character of the Psychoanalytic Situation. *J. Amer. Psychoanal. Assn.*, 23:277–299.

Mahler, M. (1968). *On Human Symbiosis and the Vicissitudes of Individuation.* New York: Int. Univ. Press.

Meltzer, D. (1984). *Dream-Life.* Perthshire: Clunie Press.

Miller, P. (2015). Piera Aulagnier, an Introduction. *Int. J. Psycho-Anal.,* 96:1355–1369.

Ogden, T. H. (1996). Reconsidering Three Aspects of Psychoanalytic Technique. *Int. J. Psycho-Anal.,* 77:883–899.

Ogden, T. H. (1997a). Reverie and Interpretation. *Psychoanal. Q.,* 66:567–595.

Ogden, T. H. (1997b). Reverie and Metaphor. *Int. J. Psycho-Anal.,* 78:719–732.

Ogden, T. H. (2001). Conversations at the Frontier of Dreaming. *Fort Da,* 7(2):7–14.

Ogden, T. H. (2003). On Not Being Able to Dream. *Int. J. Psycho-Anal.,* 84(1):17–30.

Ogden, T. H. (2007a). On Talking-as-Dreaming. *Int. J. Psycho-Anal.,* 88:575–589.

Ogden, T. H. (2007b). Elements of Analytic Style: Bion's Clinical Seminars. *Int. J. Psycho-Anal.,* 88(5):1185–1200.

Ogden, T. H. (2009). Rediscovering Psychoanalysis. *Psychoanal. Persp.,* 6:22–31.

Ogden, T. H. (2010). On Three Forms of Thinking: Magical Thinking Dream Thinking, and Transformative Thinking. *Psychoanal. Q.,* 79(2):317–347.

Ogden, T. H. (2011). Reading Susan Isaacs: Toward a Radically Revised Theory of Thinking. *Int. J. Psychoanal.,* 92: 925–942.

Ogden, T. H. (2012). How the Analyst Thinks as Clinician and as Literary Reader. *Psychoanal. Persp.,* 9:243–273.

Ogden, T. H. (2017). Dreaming the Analytic Session: A Clinical Essay. *Psychoanal Q.,* 86(1):1–20.

Oliner, M. (2013). "Non-represented" Mental States. In Levine, H. L., Reed, G. S., & Scarfone, D. (Eds.), *Unrepresented States and the Construction of Meaning.* London: Karnac.

O'Shaughnessy, E. (2005). Whose Bion?. *Int. J. Psycho-Anal.,* 86(6):1523–1528.

Paniagua, C. (2001). The Attraction of Topographical Technique. *Int. J. Psychoanal., 82*(4):671–684.

Piaget, J., & Inhelder, B. (1959). *The Psychology of the Child.* New York: Basic Books.

Pine, F. (2011). Beyond Pluaralism: Psychoanalysis and the Workings of the Mind. *Psychoanal. Q.,* 80:823–856.

Ross, W. D., & Kapp, F. T. (1962). A Technique for Self-Analysis of Countertransference— Use of the Psychoanalyst's Visual Images in Response to Patient's Dreams. *J. Amer. Psychoanal. Assn.,* 10:643–657.

Rumelhart, D. E. (1989). The Architecture of Mind: A Connectionist Approach. In *Foundations of Cognitive Science,* ed. M. A. Posner. Cambridge, MA: The MIT Press, pgs. 133–159.

Sandler, J. (1976). Dreams, Unconscious Fantasies and "Identity of Perception." *Int. Rev. Psycho-Anal.,* 3:33–42.

Schmidt-Hellerau, C. (2001). *Life Drive and Death Drive.* New York: Other Press.

Schmidt-Hellerau, C. (2005). The Door to Being Preserved and Alive. *Int. J. Psycho-Anal.,* 86:1261–1264.

Schmidt-Hellerau, C. (2006). Surviving in Absence: On The Preservative and Death Drives and Their Clinical Utility. *Psychoanal. Q.,* 75(4):1057–1095.

Schmidt-Hellerau, C. (2008). The Lethic Phallus: Rethinking the Misery of Oedipus. *Psychoanal. Q.,* 77(3):719–753.

Schmidt-Hellerau, C. (2009). "You've Hurt Me!": Clinical Reflections on Moral Sadism. *Psychoanal. Q.,* 78(1):233–241.

Smolensky, P. (1988). On the Proper Treatment of Connectionism. *Behav. & Brain Sci.,* 11:1–22, 59–74.

Spitz, R. A. (1945). Hospitalism—An Inquiry Into the Genesis of Psychiatric Conditions in Early Childhood. *Psychoanal. St. Child,* 1:53–74.

Spitz, R. A. (1946). Hospitalism—A Follow-Up Report on Investigation Described in Volume I, 1945. *Psychoanal. St. Child*, 2:113–117.

Steiner, J. (1994). Patient-Centered and Analyst-Centered Interpretations: Some Implications of Containment and Countertransference. *Psychoanal. Inq.*, 14(3):406.

Stern, D. and Sander, L. (1980). New Knowledge about the Infant from Current Research: Implications for Psychoanalysis. *J. Amer. Psychoanal. Assn.*, 28:181–198.

Taylor, D. (2011). Commentary on Vermote's 'on the Value of "Late Bion" to Analytic Theory and Practice'. *Int. J. Psycho-Anal.*, 92:1099–1112.

Vermote, R. (2011). On the Value of 'Late Bion' to Analytic Theory and Practice. *Int. J. Psycho-Anal.*, 92:1089–1098.

Weinshel, E. M. (1984). Some Observations on the Psychoanalytic Process. *Psychoanal. Q.*, 53:63–92.

Winnicott, D. W. (1965). The Maturational Processes and the Facilitating Environment. *Int. Psycho-Anal. Lib.*, 64:1–276.

Winnicott, D. W. (1987). *Babies and their Mothers*. Cambridge, MA: Persues.

INDEX

References to endnotes consist of the page number followed by the letter 'n' followed by the number of the note.